The Foolish Woman

A DAILY DEVOTIONAL

Kimberly Moses

Copyright © 2020 by **Kimberly Moses**

All rights reserved. No part of this publication may be reproduced, distributed or transmitted in any form or by any means, including photocopying, recording, or other electronic or mechanical methods, without the prior written permission of the publisher, except in the case of brief quotations embodied in critical reviews and certain other noncommercial uses permitted by copyright law. For permission requests, write to the publisher, addressed "Attention: Permissions Coordinator," at the address below.

Kimberly Moses/Rejoice Essential Publishing

PO BOX 512

Effingham, SC 29541

www.republishing.org

Unless otherwise indicated, scripture is taken from the King James Version.'

Scripture taken from the New King James Version®. Copyright © 1982 by Thomas Nelson. Used by permission. All rights reserved.

The Foolish Woman/ Kimberly Moses

ISBN-13: 978-1-952312-60-1
Library of Congress Control Number: 2021932907

Dedication

THIS BOOK WOULDN'T BE possible without the inspiration of the Holy Spirit. When I thought my life and ministry was over, He gave me another chance. I promised Him that I would help someone not to make the same mistakes. I am grateful that the Lord never gave up on me when I was at my worse.

2 Timothy 3:16-17 says, "All scripture is given by inspiration of God, and is profitable for

doctrine, for reproof, for correction, for instruction in righteousness: That the man of God may be perfect, thoroughly furnished unto all good works."

Table of Contents

ACKNOWLEDGMENTS xi
INTRODUCTION 1
CHAPTER 1:   Prayers 7
Day 1 19
Day 2 22
DAY 3 25
DAY 4 28
DAY 5 31
DAY 6 34
DAY 7 37
DAY 8 39
DAY 9 42
DAY 10 45
DAY 11 48
DAY 12 51
DAY 13 54
DAY 14 57
DAY 15 60
DAY 16 63
DAY 17 66
DAY 18 69
DAY 19 72
DAY 20 75
DAY 21 78

DAY 22	81
DAY 23	84
DAY 24	87
DAY 25	90
DAY 26	93
DAY 27	96
DAY 28	99
DAY 29	102
DAY 30	104
DAY 31	107
DAY 32	109
DAY 33	112
DAY 34	115
DAY 35	118
DAY 36	121
DAY 37	124
DAY 38	127
ABOUT THE AUTHOR	130

Acknowledgments

Thank you, Tron Moses, for being my lover and friend. I love building with you. Thanks for being with me during the good and bad times. I love you babe.

Thank you to my natural and spiritual parents. Thank you to my siblings and my children. There is nothing better than a family with whom I can be myself and truly want to see me prosper in life.

Thank you to all my supporters, friends, mentees, and my prayer family. There are too many to name individually, but I love you all.

Introduction

I CAN REMEMBER IT LIKE it was yesterday. I was sitting in jail, numb, and in disbelief. I couldn't believe that I was back in a place that I vowed never to return. "A prophet of God is here. A Christian is sitting in jail. Who will take me seriously if I try to minister to them? My ministry is over," these thoughts raced through my mind. I tried to cry, but the shock of the events that landed me a night in jail overwhelmed me. I humbled myself. I managed to get a prayer out, "Lord, I really messed up. Please forgive me. Please help me. Please set me free. Why am I here again? Please reveal it to me?" Immediately, the Lord began to take me back to my mother's womb. Anger entered in me then as she dealt with it. I saw flashbacks of me fighting little kids in my neighborhood and hurting others. At that moment, I laid hands on my belly and did self-deliverance. "Come out- anger that came through the womb in the name of Jesus." Suddenly, I started yawning and couldn't stop doing it for a few minutes. Tears started to stream down my face. I began to feel so light and knew that the spirit of anger came out of me. I began to hear the Lord speak to me, "Your ministry is not over. I will still use you. Things will be restored in your life. Trust me." I was thankful that the Lord had forgiven me and had to use my faith to believe the Word of the Lord regardless of what was occurring in the natural world. I began to get the download for this book to help women who are living foolishly.

"Lord, I need to get out of here but don't know who to call. My family doesn't live around here." The Lord spoke, "Call the bail bonds agent that starts with an R." A few hours later, the correctional officer let me out of my cell to make a phone call. There was a list of phone numbers of bail bonds agents taped to the wall. There had to be around 100 phone numbers. I scanned the list and saw that there was only one bail bonds-

Introduction

man listed that started with an R. I picked up the phone and dialed. "Hello. I am in jail for domestic violence. I don't have any cash on me, but I can pay you electronically. Can you help?" "Yes, I can help. That is fine. What time is your court case and has your bail been set?" he asked. I answered him with all the details and a few hours later, he bailed me out of jail. I had to spend $500, which I could've used for bills and other expenses.

Foolish choices result in devastating consequences. Perhaps you can relate to my testimony. If so, then you know that getting into trouble can be expensive because you have to pay attorneys, court costs, fees, bail, etc. Have you ever said or done something that you later regretted? We all have acted foolishly at times. In those moments, we get out of character while bringing embarrassment to ourselves and others. If we do have a relationship with the Lord, then He is grieved by our actions. I'm blessed to be a recipient of God's mercy. He allowed me to recover all as He restored me.

THE FOOLISH WOMAN

We have an enemy (devil) that loves it when we mess up and destroy our own lives. Everything isn't his fault. We have to look in the mirror and take responsibility. Some of us have pride, rebellion, dishonor, anger, bitterness, or unforgiveness in our hearts that we need to be delivered from. We have to cry out to the Lord and confess that we are that same foolish woman. We need to repent of our sins and ask the Lord for forgiveness. Then we need to go through the deliverance process.

Consider the following Scripture:
Proverbs 14:1 says, "Every wise woman buildeth her house, but the foolish plucketh it down with her own hands."

I was this foolish woman who tore down her own home with my bare hands. I hurt my ex-husband. I divided our family. I tore up property and spent money recklessly that I could've invested. At that time, I lacked the wisdom to build my house. We have to ask God for wisdom and He will give us a generous amount (James 1:5). Had I been wise, then I could've had more money in the bank, debts paid off, and a happy

Introduction

family. The Lord also showed me that our house is also referring to our bodies. For instance, when a demon is cast out of a person, they seek a dry place. When they can't find anywhere, they return to the person. If they find the house swept clean, they bring back seven spirits stronger than themselves.

Matthew 12:43-45(NKJV) says, 43 "When an unclean spirit goes out of a man, he goes through dry places, seeking rest, and finds none. 44 Then he says, 'I will return to my house from which I came.' And when he comes, he finds it empty, swept, and put in order. 45 Then he goes and takes with him seven other spirits more wicked than himself, and they enter and dwell there; and the last state of that man is worse than the first. So shall it also be with this wicked generation."

These Scriptures explain why some of us are bound and in need of deliverance. We have to get the anger, pride, and other things out of us. Our bodies are the temple of the Holy Spirit and only His Spirit shall dwell in us.

THE FOOLISH WOMAN

The purpose of this book is to bring healing and deliverance from doing foolish things. The fact that you have this book is an indication that you want help. You probably feel tired of doing crazy things and going through the same cycles. God uses books through His servants to bring restoration. This book doesn't replace the Bible, but it can be used as a complement to it. Some Scriptures might be highlighted to you by the Spirit of God. The Lord may lead you to do a further study on the subject. I will share various testimonies and provide daily prayers. You can read this book straight through or you can read daily as a devotional. You will realize that it's not just about you. Many people are depending on you and the Lord has need of you. You will start to think about your actions and the consequences and walk in a manner that's worthy of the Lord. I declare that you are no longer a foolish woman but a wise one.

CHAPTER 1

Prayers

Lord, bless me to build my house.

I decree that I will not tear down my own house.

I declare that I will be a good steward of what you have given me.

Lord, give me wisdom so I can make better choices in life.

I will keep my deliverance in Jesus' name.

I will not go backward in life in Jesus' name.

Lord, order my steps.

I bind up foolery, in Jesus' name.

THE FOOLISH WOMAN

I will not allow the devil to use me.

I bind up demonic cycles, in Jesus' name.

I will not grow weary of doing the right thing.

Lord, I will keep Your commandments.

Lord, I will not behave foolishly and grieve Your Spirit.

I will keep Your Word in my heart, in Jesus' name.

I will not speak foolishly.

Lord, guard my mouth.

I will not sin against God with my lips.

I bind up impatience.

I will wait on the Lord's promises.

Lord, create a pure heart within me.

Prayers

Lord, soften my heart.

Lord, purge me and remove anything wicked that would attach itself to me.

I will not take the bait of the enemy.

I will not be hasty.

I will not get outside of Your will.

Lord, the foolish shall not stand in Your sight.

I bind up anything that is causing distance between God and me.

God, You despise sin.

Bless me to love what You love and hate what You hate.

It's foolish to deny You Lord. I know that You are real.

The Foolish Woman

Lord, remove every hindrance to my growth in You.

Remove every stumbling block in my path.

Deliver me from all my transgression.

Don't let me be a reproach to the foolish.

Lord bless me with wisdom to handle finances.

Lord bless me with wisdom so I can leave my family an inheritance.

Bless me with wisdom when it comes to marriages.

Bless me with wisdom when it comes to ministry.

Bless me with wisdom when it comes to business.

I will think about what I say before I speak.

God, You know my heart and thoughts. Remove any foolish thing from me.

Prayers

I decree that I will not sin against You by thinking the wrong things.

I will not be ignorant and do things that grieve Your Spirit.

I bind up foolish actions that will cause my body to be afflicted.

I bind up foolishness that results in premature death.

I bind up foolish mistakes that result in scandals.

I bind up foolery that will cause me to hit rock bottom.

I bind up being careless that will cause me to stumble.

Lord, increase my discernment.

Lord, block access to agents of Satan from entering my life.

THE FOOLISH WOMAN

Lord, I will not despise Your wisdom and instruction.

I am in awe of You God, so I will not sin against You.

Lord, give me insight, so I know what to do in every situation.

Lord, it's foolish to deny Your existence.

Lord, I will not reject the counsel of the people that You send to help me.

I will separate myself from toxic people and environments because they will bring me down.

I will be humble and be obedient to Your Word.

I will not be a scorner.

I will remain teachable.

I will not make silly mistakes that will cause me to be demoted in life.

Prayers

I will not make silly mistakes that will cause me and my loved ones shame.

I will not disgrace the body of Christ.

I will forsake being foolish.

I will go in the way of understanding.

I will stay on the straight and narrow path.

I don't know everything, so I will always posture myself to be forever learning.

I will not reject the people that You sent to bless me.

I will not be clamorous.

I will not be quick to react.

Lord, embed Your Word in my heart, so I don't sin against You.

I will not be a prating fool.

THE FOOLISH WOMAN

I won't treat life as a game.

I bind up foolishness that causes sorrow.

I won't be naïve and think that my good looks will save me from facing the consequences of my actions.

Destruction will not be my portion.

I will be like the wise men and lay up knowledge.

I will not dig myself deeper into a pit.

I will not hide hatred with lying lips.

I will not utter slander.

I will walk in the Spirit, so I don't fulfill the lust of the flesh.

I will follow the Spirit of Truth.

I will be an honest person.

I will have compassion.

Prayers

I will be known for having integrity.

I will not be wise in my own eyes.

I will hearken unto wise counsel.

I will let go of offenses and forgive.

My wrath will not be known.

I will keep my business private.

I will not put my personal business on my social media networks.

Lord, give me discernment on who to trust.

I will not be connected to the wrong people.

I will shun foolish counsel.

I will not proclaim foolishness.

I will not love drama.

THE FOOLISH WOMAN

I will not have a rod of pride in my mouth.

I will not stir up strife and make matters worse.

I will depart from evil and will not let anger consume me.

Lord, let Your wisdom rest upon me.

I will not use wicked devices.

Lord, give me the tongue of the wise.

I will not despise my parents' instruction.

Lord, don't allow me to bring my parents sorrow.

Lord, bless my children never to bring me sorrow.

I will hold my peace and let You avenge me.

I will close my mouth and put down my ego.

I will honor leadership.

Prayers

I will not make a mess of things.

My lips will not be the snare of my soul.

I will speak life and not death.

My heart will not fret against the Lord.

I will not walk in a spirit of perversion.

I will not be found meddling.

I will cease from strife.

I will not speak in the ears of a fool.

I will not waste time or energy on foolish people.

I will not answer a fool according to his folly.

I will walk away if necessary during an escalated disagreement.

I will not be like a dog that returns to his own vomit.

The Foolish Woman

I will not return to folly.

I will not keep going around the mountain.

Anger will not rest in my bosom.

I will renew my mind.

I will not be wicked.

I will not make evil plans.

No one will ever bewitch me.

I will never follow someone to hell.

I will not be bamboozled by the enemy.

I will never be a part of a cult.

I will set my mind on Jesus Christ.

I will walk circumspectly.

DAY 1

Today's Verse

1 SAMUEL 13:13 SAYS, "AND Samuel said to Saul, Thou hast done foolishly: thou hast not kept the commandment of the LORD thy God, which he commanded thee: for now would the LORD have established thy kingdom upon Israel for ever."

In 1 Samuel 13, Saul and his men were in battle. There were 6,000 Philistines with 3000 chariots. They were ready to attack Saul and the Israelites. Saul's men were afraid, so they hid in caves and bushes among the cliff. Samuel told Saul that he would meet in him seven days to make a burnt offering unto God before the battle. Samuel came a little late and Saul had already burnt the offering himself. Saul acted very foolishly because he grew impatient with waiting on

THE FOOLISH WOMAN

Samuel and took matters into his own hands. He was out of order because only the priest was authorized to burn offerings. Samuel declares that God would take the kingdom away from him and find him a replacement.

How many times have you grown impatient and took matters into your own hands? You grew tired of waiting on God and did something foolish. Perhaps you entered a wrong relationship, fell into sin, and settled. Once you got outside of the will of God, you realized that you really messed up. It's foolish to do something that God never authorized for your life. Saul lost his kingdom over it. Many people have forfeited the blessings of the Lord due to poor decisions. We have to wait on the Lord even when it appears easier to find a way out or settle for something less than God's best. Saul failed to realize that God allowed a delay to test what was really in his heart. Consider that God is testing your motives when things get delayed. Will you lose your faith and do something foolish if what you are waiting for doesn't arrive on time? Or will you trust God and be patient and stay in His will?

Today's Verse

PRAYER:

Dear Heavenly Father,

I humble myself and repent for taking matters into my own hands. I bind up being impatient and pray that you bless me with patience, which is one of the fruits of the Holy Spirit (Galatians 5). I don't want to miss out on the promises You have for my life because I have done something foolish. Lord, bless me to please You and stay in your will. I don't want to do something that You haven't authorized. I pray that my motives are pure and pleasing in Your sight. Thank you for answering this prayer, in Jesus' name. Amen.

DAY 2

Today's Verse

Job 2:10 says, "But he said unto her, Thou speakest as one of the foolish women speaketh. What? Shall we receive good at the hand of God, and shall we not receive evil? In all this did not Job sin with his lips.

Job was a devout man and he truly loved God. He would often offer burnt offerings to God for his children. One day Satan approached God. God asked, "Have you noticed my servant Job? There is no one like him on the earth." Satan said, "Well, he will curse you to your face if you allow everything that he owns to be destroyed." God gave Satan permission to cause chaos in Job's life but told him to spare his life. Well, after Job's children and livestock died, and he was smitten with painful boils upon his body, his wife spoke as a foolish woman. Job knew better and never cursed God regardless of what his wife said and what the devil was doing.

Many of us have been like Job's wife. We have spoken things out of what we saw and felt. We didn't recognize that the devil was using our mouths to destroy someone's life. Had Job listened, then we would have never received double for his trouble (Job 42). The words "foolish women" in Hebrew is Nabal. In other words, what his wife spoke was stupid, wicked, and vile. We can't lose touch with the reality that God will come through for us one day. We can't blurt anything out that comes to our mind. Cursing God is a sin and, sadly, many do it. They take the name of the Lord in vain. Exodus 20:7 commands us not to use the Lord's name in vain and this verse warns us that we will be judged if we do it. Don't take the enemy's bait of sinning with your mouth. Don't shorten your life or cause judgment to come upon you by cursing God. Don't be a stumbling block to someone else by giving lousy counsel.

PRAYER:

Dear Heavenly Father,

Lord, I love You with my whole heart. Give me the wisdom to speak and counsel others in a way that glorifies You. I hate to see the people I love suffer. Even though I may mean well, I must make sure that my advice lines up with Your Word. I refused to allow the devil to speak through me. I declare that I will never be a spawn of Satan. I don't want to speak as a foolish woman. I don't want to speak stupid, wicked, and vile things. Lord, bless my heart to be pure because out of the abundance of the heart the mouth speaks, in Jesus' name. Amen.

DAY 3

Today's Verse

Psalm 5:5 says, "The foolish shall not stand in thy sight: thou hatest all workers of iniquity."

This Psalm is a prayer from David. He was suffering persecution and cried out to the Lord. He put the Lord in remembrance of love for him. He believed that God was going to protect him. God loves everyone, but He hates sin. The word foolish in this verse means arrogant or boastful. These people are unteachable and brag about their own strength instead of God's. These types of people will not stand in the Lord's presence because they are sinful. God is omnipresent, but His Spirit doesn't rest or dwell everywhere. Holiness attracts His presence. God takes no pleasure in the wicked, but He delights in the righteous.

Have you ever been in warfare where you seemed to be attacked on every side? I felt like David, where I cried day and night. I didn't understand why some people hated me for no reason. They hated Jesus within me. At the darkest moment, I learned to get in God's presence to comfort my soul. I would wait in the Lord's presence to see or hear what He would tell me. I knew that in His presence is the fullest of joy and my place of refuge. Miraculously, God protected me from my enemies. He continued to bless me, the more my enemies tried to curse me. The enemy can't curse what God has blessed. God strengthened me to go forth in ministry.

PRAYER:

Dear Heavenly Father,

Thank You for protecting me. I know that I am Your child and You will vindicate me. You will right all my wrongs. You will make every crooked place straight. You will make the rough

Today's Verse

places smooth. I decree that I will live holy as You are holy. I repent for any pride, rebellion, or boasting in my own strengths instead of Yours. I will humble myself and You will exalt me in due season. I will not grieve Your presence by behaving foolishly. Thank You for answering this prayer in Jesus' name. Amen.

DAY 4

Today's Verse

Psalm 14:1 says, "The fool hath said in his heart, There is no God. They are corrupt. They have done abominable works. There is none that doeth good.

When you look at the oceans, mountains, trees, sky, sun, moon, stars, creatures, and so on, you will know that a mighty Creator crafted these things. When you go through trials in life, God warns sinners and His children to watch out for impending danger by speaking directly to us, giving a dream, or sending a message across our path. Even if you didn't know God, you would know that He exists by looking at the blessedness of His people. One of my pet peeves is when someone says, "A voice told me this or that." It was God who warned them and spared their lives from harm. God deserves the glory. A foolish person will deny all of these things and confess there is no God.

Sometimes when I minister online, trolls will come on my videos. They will say all kinds of blasphemy. They will say that, "There is no God. The Holy Spirit isn't real. Speaking in tongues is false. People are lying about getting healed. I am delusional, etc." I don't argue with them. I continue to preach the Gospel in hopes that seeds are watered or planted. Sadly, these people will suffer eternal damnation if they never accept Jesus into their hearts. They don't realize that Satan has blinded their hearts and minds (2 Corinthians 4:4), where they can't see the truth of the Gospel of Jesus Christ.

PRAYER:

Dear Heavenly Father,

I know that You are real. It is a foolish thing to deny Your existence. Deepen our connection and allow me to feel Your tangible presence daily. I can never deny You when I behold creation and all the wonders upon the earth. If it weren't for You, then I would be dead, in jail, or in a mental institution. Thank You for all the times You protected me. Thank You for everything that You have done for me. Give me wisdom and show me how to minister to the unbeliever effectively. You said that He who wins souls is wise. Thank You for answering this prayer in Jesus' name. Amen.

DAY 5

Today's Verse

Psalm 39:8 says, "Deliver me from all my transgressions: make me not the reproach of the foolish."

David was in a place of repentance. He asked the Lord to cover his sins and deliver him so the foolish people would not mock him. David didn't want to give his enemies any room to say anything about him. Some people are waiting for your downfall so they can laugh. We shouldn't rejoice when our enemies stumble but pray for God's mercy concerning them. Not everyone follows God's commands, so they are glad when you get exposed. God is merciful and He gives us multiple chances to get it right privately. When we see a public scandal, it is most likely because the minister has ignored the Lord's correction for a period. Their sins caught up with them.

Years ago, I was in school full-time, pursuing to become a medical doctor. Everyone looked at me and saw my determination. They thought I had the perfect marriage and life. They didn't know that my life was in shambles until the divorce became public and I was arrested. I lost myself and found myself arguing in front of people. I didn't care about what people thought. It wasn't until reality set in or when I started to feel the consequences of my sins that I felt shame. I was hurt by some people who I thought cared for me by the things they said about me. My mistakes being on public display gave my enemies something to talk about. After I repented and allowed the Lord to do a great work in my life, my name and character were restored. The Lord covered my sin and delivered me so I would not be a reproach to the foolish.

PRAYER:

Dear Heavenly Father,

Today's Verse

I humble myself and repent for being foolish. I apologize for taking matters into my own hands. Lord, deliver me from all my transgressions. I am tired of repeating cycles. Break every demonic stronghold and set me free. Lord, spare me from shame and the embarrassment of my enemies, knowing my shortcomings. Purify me so I can truly walk in a manner that is worthy of You. My life is not my own. I belong to You. Thank You for Your transformative power working in my life, in Jesus' name. Amen.

DAY 6

Today's Verse

Psalm 49:10 says, "For he seeth that wise men die, likewise the fool and the brutish person perish, and leave their wealth to others."

When we die, we can't take our money with us. Money can't save us from death or buy us salvation. Wise and foolish men both will die one day. Death is something that we all will experience. We will not be on this earth forever because our life is like a vapor (James 4:14). It's a high probability that the foolish and stupid person will perish without leaving any wealth to others. Contrarily the wise men will leave an inheritance to their children's children (Proverbs 13:22). We must think about our legacies.

Today's Verse

Many foolish people left their wealth to strangers throughout history because they had an ought with their family members. As a result, long-lasting legal battles occurred while the family and strangers fought over the dead person's assets. A wise person wouldn't want to put burdens upon their family. They want their memory to be a good one instead of one of turmoil. Some don't leave a will and feel like it's bad to leave an inheritance or wealth for their loved ones.

PRAYER:

Dear Heavenly Father,

I realize that I will not live forever on this earth. Bless me to have my priorities together and make preparations for my family. I never want to be a burden on anyone. Bless my family and me to get life insurance and draft our last will and testament. I don't want my family to be fighting over any assets that I own, so give me wisdom. Allow me to choose and determine who gets what from me. I want my family to be successful and I will gladly pass the torch to them when it's time. Lord, bless me to leave a great legacy that will glorify You in Jesus' name. Amen.

DAY 7

Today's Verse

PSALM 69:5 SAYS, "O God, thou knowest my foolishness; and my sins are not hid from thee."

God knows our strengths and weaknesses. When He created us, He was very strategic on how we would look, our personalities, and our assignment in life. He sees us and what we do when no one is around. If we sin, then He knows what we did. If our hearts aren't pure in His sight, we can't pretend that we are in right standing with Him. Many are confessing they love the Lord but their actions are contrary. Some are acting foolish Monday through Saturday. Then they act like a Saint on Sunday. What is done in the dark will be revealed in the light.

THE FOOLISH WOMAN

Years ago, I was in an adulterous relationship. It was very foolish because I was destroying my family. I had everything: career, house, marriage, kids, money, etc but I didn't appreciate it. I wasn't content and I was backslidden. I tore down my home by allowing the enemy to use me. I didn't resist temptation but let it consume me. It wasn't until I became severely tormented by demonic spirits that I stopped sinning. I repented and God knew when I was sincere. He was so kind that He delivered me.

PRAYER:

Dear Heavenly Father,

You are mighty and deserve all the glory. I can't hide anything from You. Deliver me from sin and any foolery in my life. I don't want to be a hypocrite. You see my motives and what's in my heart. It's not worth sinning against you. Let me be pleasing in Your sight. Order my steps and strengthen me in Your Word so I don't give in to temptation. Thank you for answering this prayer in Jesus' name. Amen.

DAY 8

Today's Verse

PSALM 73:22 SAYS, "So foolish was I, and ignorant: I was as a beast before thee."

Asaph was jealous of the wicked because he was suffering and going through trials. It seemed like the wicked were prospering and Asaph wanted to speak what was in his heart. However, he didn't because he knew that he would've let people down. It wasn't until he went to the temple of the Lord that he realized he was acting foolishly in his thoughts and being in his emotions. He realized that the wicked will perish and will not spend eternity with God. He compares himself to an animal because they aren't even aware of God or eternal life.

I learned never to compare myself. Celebrities seem happy, but some aren't. Their marriages are on the brink of destruction. Some are on drugs, etc. Some don't have the peace that we have because they don't have a relationship with Jesus, the Prince of Peace. Sadly they are on a path of destruction and a very few people find the path of life (Matthew 7:13-14). We, as humans, have dominion over the creatures of the earth (Genesis 1:26-28). We are deemed more intelligent. The lilies of the field and the birds in the sky (Matthew 6:25-34) aren't concerned about God or spreading the Gospel. We have a huge responsibility and shouldn't take it lightly.

PRAYER:

Dear Heavenly Father,

I repent from envying the wicked and becoming discouraged about it. I won't try to keep up with the Jones' just to be seen, popular, or famous. I will not compare myself to others. I just want to be pleasing in your sight. Even when I get in my feelings, I will not speak them out and sin against You with my lips. I choose to praise You Lord instead of complaining. I will worship You and enjoy fellowshipping. I know You are faithful, so it's a matter of time before the promises over my life manifest. Thank You for answering this prayer, in Jesus' name. Amen.

DAY 9

Today's Verse

*P*SALM 107:17 SAYS, "FOOLS because of their transgression, and because of their iniquities, are afflicted.

Foolish people make dangerous mistakes that jeopardize their health. They sleep around or have unprotected sex, which leads them to sin against their own bodies (1 Corinthians 6:18), ungodly soul ties, children out of wedlock, and various STDs. Some may do drugs or drink a lot of alcohol, causing HIV, Hepatitis, heart attacks, cirrhosis, organ failure, and other afflictions. Others may get caught up in doing illegal activities that make them a target of gun violence, murder, or danger. Sin equals death (Romans 6:23).

Today's Verse

Years ago, my friends and I lived a promiscuous lifestyle. She ended up getting herpes and I was infected with many other STDs. We were very young at the time and not saved. Our sin caused our bodies to be afflicted. I was at risk of having cervical cancer because my pap-smear tests came back with a negative report. I had to go to the gynecologist and Iodine was placed upon my cervix. After that, my tests were great. I realized that sleeping around was not worth it. After I got saved, I waited on marriage to be intimate with my husband.

PRAYER:

Dear Heavenly Father,

I repent for doing foolish things that were afflicting my body. Sin does equal death. If You spare my life in the natural, then the sin results in spiritual death. I don't want to cut my life short or die prematurely due to poor decisions. I don't want to nail Jesus back on the cross by living a reckless life. I don't want to backslide. I rededicate my life to You, Lord. Please order my steps. Thank You for answering this prayer in Jesus' name. Amen.

DAY 10

Today's Verse

PROVERBS 1:7 SAYS, "THE fear of the Lord is the beginning of knowledge: but fools despise wisdom and instruction."

Whenever the fear of the Lord is present in our hearts, we are aware of sin. We will become more afraid of our Creator's judgment than man's opinions. His fear, which translates to being in awe of Him, is why we don't want to grieve His Holy Spirit. When we acknowledge God and become aware of His presence, we seek Him first. As a result, He gives us godly wisdom for growth and knowledge in what He is calling us to do. However, fools hate wisdom and instructions and feel like they know everything.

Sadly, most fall straight upon their faces due to pride.

God places mentors in our lives to help us on this journey. They have been places that we have never gone. They have experiences that will be beneficial to us if we can learn the same lessons they did. We have to pray for God to send the right people, mentors, and leaders into our life. Contrarily, we have to pray for the wrong people to be removed. If we receive godly counsel, then we will be spared heartache, pain, and shame. I am thankful for my mentors because as I followed their counsel, I went to another level.

PRAYER:

Dear Heavenly Father,

I thank You for placing the right people in my life and removing the wrong ones. I will be humble and see the person's heart to receive the counsel that you gave them for me. I am in awe of You and when You are in first place, everything else will line up. I won't try to build or do things in my own strength and wisdom. How-

Today's Verse

ever, I will seek You and get divine counsel to stay in alignment with Your will. Thank You for answering this prayer, in Jesus' name. Amen.

DAY 11

Today's Verse

Proverbs 1:22 says, "How long, ye simple ones, will ye love simplicity? And the scorners delight in their scorning, and fools hate knowledge?"

Fools are compared to simpletons or immature ones. They make fun of others who show more maturity and they treat life as a game. There is a time to be serious and a time to play. We have to discern the two. For instance, when it's time to work or learn, we must be serious, especially when working for God. However, in our season of rest or leisure time, we can relax, joke around, and take our minds off stressors. Imagine someone joking around during a team collaboration, test, meeting, etc. Then they mock

Today's Verse

the person who is advancing or knowledgeable in a particular area they should be learning from. You probably would get annoyed and feel like that individual isn't taking the opportunity seriously, not paying attention, and won't contribute anything of value.

Years ago, I was very immature and didn't consider the consequences of my actions. I would speak my mind, fight, curse people out, engage in dangerous behavior, and felt like I knew everything. I was so used to being in control that my plans went out the window when I went through a wilderness season. Nothing I tried to do worked. I began to panic and became depressed. I went to a secular counselor who brought out the fact that I was reacting too fast without processing things. She gave me a workbook that helped me not to allow emotions to run my life. During the same time, I went to a Christian counselor who incorporated God's Word into counseling. I began to see many attributes of myself that I didn't like and I drew closer to the Lord. I sought the Lord and heard Him tell me, "Grow up!" Those words changed my life and I started taking heed to counsel to make better decisions in life.

PRAYER:

Dear Heavenly Father,

I humble myself and repent for any time that I didn't take opportunities or life seriously when I needed to do so. I repent for wasting time and not being a good steward over what You have given me. I repent for procrastinating and being disobedient. If I have offended anyone with selfish and foolish behaviors, I pray that they can forgive me. I will remain teachable and mature into who You are calling me to be. I will be about Your business and make You proud. Thank You for answering this prayer, in Jesus' name. Amen.

DAY 12

Today's Verse

Proverbs 3:35 says, "The wise shall inherit glory: but shame shall be the promotion of fools."

Wise people will make better decisions that will preserve their lives. They will have discernment and not connect with the wrong crowd. They will be great stewards of their finances and build wealth. You will see God continually promote them in life. The blessings and favor of the Lord are evident for all to witness. On the other hand, a foolish person will experience shame due to poor decision making. Their sins and stupid mistakes will catch up to them. For a season, it seemed like they were getting away with things. Now what was done in the darkness is coming to light.

THE FOOLISH WOMAN

I experienced shame when my first marriage fell apart. For years, I was pretending to be someone I wasn't. I was going through the motions of church. The sermon went into one ear and out the other. I didn't take notes or apply what was taught. I only went to please my husband at the time because he was an idol. I drank alcohol, watched porn, read a daily horoscope, didn't pray, or read the Bible. My heart was hard towards God and anger consumed me. I destroyed property and had to pay restitution. I moved out of a five bedroom house into a small one bedroom apartment. I couldn't use the college degrees that I have worked hard to obtain over the years because I had criminal charges against me. I was being demoted in life due to poor choices. I felt like I should've been further along in life and that I was going backward. However, when I yielded to God, He accelerated some things in and through me. I was able to do things in a short amount of time which should've taken years.

PRAYER:

Today's Verse

Dear Heavenly Father,

I bless Your name. I ask that You order my steps and allow me to have an ear to hear Your counsel. Bless me with wisdom from on high. I don't want a demotion but a promotion in every area of my life. Take me through the process of allowing me to be a carrier of Your glory. I declare instead of shame, I will receive a double portion of honor. Lord, bless me with a supernatural acceleration to catch up on things that I should've done years ago. Thank You for Your grace, mercy, favor, provision, protection, guidance, and strength. I love You Lord. Thanks for answering this prayer, in Jesus' name. Amen.

DAY 13

Today's Verse

Proverbs 9:6 says, "Forsake the foolish, and live; and go in the way of the understanding."

It's better to shun evil and dismiss pride. What do you have to prove? We must be secure in who God is calling us to be? We have to be hidden in Christ and dead to ourselves. Just because it seems like a way is popular doesn't mean that it's the right path. Popularity doesn't mean God is in it. We must follow the Lord's path or the way of the understanding. We have the Holy Spirit within us and if something doesn't agree with Him, then we must take heed. That is why we have checks in our spirits to warn us that we are heading down the wrong path.

Today's Verse

I remember being very confrontational and felt like I had to prove how crazy I could become if someone did or said anything against me. I didn't realize that watching certain reality shows embedded anger deep within me. I found out that one of my co-workers in the hospital was gossiping about me. I was furious and I planned to show out. I thought it over in my mind. "Ok, if she gets loud, then I will pick up a chair and throw it at her." I saw her in the hallway and asked, "I heard what you have been saying about me. If you have anything to say, then say it to my face. I am right here." She looked at me and said, "I don't want any problems," and walked away. I was stunned because she forsook the foolish. A soft answer turns away wrath (Proverbs 15:1). I thank God that things went the opposite of my plans because I could've been arrested, banned from working in the hospital, and lost my license to practice.

PRAYER:

Dear Heavenly Father,

The Foolish Woman

I repent for feeling like I need to prove myself. I am not fighting against flesh and blood. But I am fighting against principalities, powers, rulers of darkness, and hosts of wickedness. I yield this flesh to You and permit You to kill it. Get any pride out of me. Keep me from doing foolish things. I will not avenge myself but allow You to. I will not take matters into my own hands. I will not grieve Your Spirit because I feel like I have to prove my point. I will be silent when people gossip about me on the job, on social media, in church, etc. I know that if I will be still, trust You, then You will fight for me. Thank You for answering this prayer, in Jesus' name. Amen.

DAY 14

Today's Verse

Proverbs 9:13 says, "A foolish woman is clamorous; she is simple and knoweth nothing."

Foolishness can be compared to a loud woman who is noisy, ghetto, mean spirited, etc. She thinks by acting like this that she is showing people that she doesn't play or take any crap. However, she is ignorant and doesn't even know it. In certain settings, we can't be ghetto but must have class. Some black women are categorized as being angry. There aren't many black women in certain circles, jobs, or spheres for this reason. Black women must stand together and break the cycle or stigma. They don't realize that they are behaving how society has deemed them to act. They are doing more harm than good. People are watching and forming their opinions. It's wrong to categorize certain types of people into one category. For instance, it's not true to say that all men are dogs. There are some great men out there who aren't cheaters.

In 2020, after cops murdered George Floyd, many looters went rampant, tearing up businesses and stealing. I was so grieved and I knew it was wrong. God commands us not to steal and be angry and sin not. Burning down a business is wrong. That person has a family and they need to eat. I posted on my social media networks how looting was wrong and was disappointed by some of the comments I received. People felt like looting was right because they were angry. They felt like cops didn't deserve to be paid. They felt like violent protests were the answer and the police needed to pay for the injustice. I told them that not all police are bad and that God will vindicate them. People angrily said, "Wow. I am shocked that you are using your platform to talk about police and political matters." It was like they wanted me to be that angry black woman. They wanted me to be upset and praise the looters, but I refused to do so. I explained to these people that we have to be on the Lord's side and what is wrong is wrong no matter what the circumstance. We can't allow our circumstances to dictate if we are going to follow God's commands.

PRAYER:

Dear Heavenly Father,

I realize that I don't know everything. You can use anyone to show me new things. It doesn't matter if I agree with it or not. You are sovereign and You know what You are doing. I will not be clamorous and be a reproach to myself. Being loud doesn't mean that I am powerful in You. The meek or those who are gentle in spirit will inherit the earth. I want to be someone who will inherit all the promises that You have for them, Lord. I am tired of going through the same cycles. Deliver and set me free, God. Thank You for answering this prayer in Jesus' name. Amen.

DAY 15

Today's Verses

Proverbs 10:8,10, "The wise in heart will receive commandments: but a prating fool shall fall...He that winketh with the eye causeth sorrow: but a prating fool shall fall."

Wise people will do what they are told and it won't take them long to grasp the instructions. Also, a wink may get you into trouble. We can't use our looks to get us out of trouble. However, foolish people will keep talking, digging themselves deeper into a pit. A prating fool talks for a long time and doesn't know when to keep quiet. As a result, they will experience much sorrow. For instance, people are being killed by crooked police for talking too much. Some of those wicked cops are trigger happy and will gladly say that a person is noncompliant or resisting arrest. God will put a bridle on our mouths so we can only edify grace unto the hearer.

Years ago, I was an exotic dancer and a hustler. I knew how to talk anyone out of things to get what I wanted. I depended on my good looks to get me out of trouble. I had a spirit of seduction and would do anything to get my way. I made promises that I couldn't keep and I would avoid people that I wronged. I was a prating fool. God showed me that you could be beautiful on the outside but ugly on the inside. You can't buy your way out of everything. We have to follow God's commands and the laws of the land. God is a God of order. We must realize that these laws are in place for protection.

PRAYER:

Dear Heavenly Father,

I love You, so I will follow Your commands. I don't want to be a prating fool. I will use manners and speech in a way that pleases You. I will talk in a way that edifies grace to the hearer. I will not use my body or looks to compromise. I will be a great representation of Jesus Christ. Lord, bless my feet not to stumble. Keep me on the straight and narrow path. Thank You for answering this prayer, in Jesus' name. Amen.

DAY 16

Today's Verse:

Proverbs 10:14 says, "Wise men lay up knowledge but the mouth of the foolish is near destruction."

A wise person is constantly learning and will search out a matter about a particular subject. For instance, if God is calling someone to start a business, then a wise person will invest in books, training, seminars, etc., to learn what they can to excel in their field. That's what I did when God told me to start a publishing business. However, a foolish person will be lazy and won't take the time to do what's necessary for their growth. They won't appreciate the people that God sent in their lives to be a blessing unto them. We must realize that we aren't self-sufficient. We need one another and God uses people to bless us.

When I was in the wilderness, I needed money for food, rent, utilities, and other expenses. I was so used to having money in my account and getting whatever I wanted from various stores. However, those days were over and I needed help. At first, I was too prideful and embarrassed that I refused offers for help. Some people asked me if I needed anything and I said no. I didn't realize how stubborn I was, so it took my account being hundreds of dollars in the negative, no gas money, an empty pantry, and overdue bills to accept help. I repented for allowing shame to cloud my judgment. God used this situation to humble me and to receive whoever and whatever He sends to sustain me.

PRAYER:

Dear Heavenly Father,

I thank You for being gracious and loving. You know how to chastise me so I can get back on track. You are so faithful and constantly look-

Today's Verse:

ing out for me. I may not understand why I go through certain trials, but I know You will reveal the reason in time. Bless me with wisdom in the storm and allow me to learn the lesson, so I don't prolong the process. I pray that I will be like the wise men who lay up knowledge and understand what You want me to do. Help me to humble myself, so pride doesn't stop the blessings You have for my life. Thank You for answering this prayer, in Jesus' name. Amen.

DAY 17

Today's Verse

Proverbs 10:18 says, "He that hideth hatred with lying lips, and he that uttereth a slander, is a fool."

It's dangerous being around a person who hates you but pretends like they don't. They can't be trusted because they will be around you to gather information so they can use it against you. We have to pray for God to remove the wrong people from our lives. Some people aren't for us and they will be exposed over time. It's a foolish thing to spread gossip because you don't know if it's a lie. Whenever we tell lies, we allow the devil to use us because he is the father of all lies (John 8:44).

Today's Verse

When I was a teenager, I was hanging out at my best friend's house one day. Many girls hated us and always tried to fight us. My friend wasn't a fighter, but I was, so I often defended her. As a result, those girls left my friend alone but hated me even more. A girl came over, but she was really two-faced. She laughed, ate snacks, and watched TV with us. We actually had a great time. However, the next day, false rumors started to spread around the school that she went over to my friend's house and saw us having sex. I was furious because she was trying to ruin our reputations. After school, I grabbed a paring knife and took my friend along to this girl's house to confront her. I knocked on her door and asked for something to drink. She gave me a big cup of soda. I splashed it in her face and stomped her a few times, then ran. My friend followed behind me. As a result, my friend and I had to do a hundred hours of community service, which was humiliating for me. I learned to let people talk and allow God to fight my battles because there will always be someone who doesn't like you.

PRAYER:

THE FOOLISH WOMAN

Dear Heavenly Father,

Let me live a lifestyle that is pleasing to you. I don't want the enemy to use me. I refuse to hate anyone. So if there is jealousy in my heart, please get it out. I bless the person who I might not favor and I let go of any insecurities and offenses. I pray they succeed. I don't want to be a phony person but one who demonstrates Your love for others. I will not spread gossip or lies about someone. Instead, I will pray for them because You love them and You want the best for them. I will let you fight my battles so I won't get in Your way. Thank You for answering this prayer, in Jesus' name. Amen.

DAY 18

Today's Verse

Proverbs 12:15 says, "The way of a fool is right in his own eyes: but he that hearkeneth unto counsel is wise."

No one knows everything and we will often face situations when we don't know what to do. Challenges will arise in business, ministry, family, workplace, etc. We can never feel like we have it all together. It's when we are the weakest God is the strongest (2 Corinthians 12:10). We have to stop and seek God for the solution. We may hear His voice or He may send someone to speak to us. Be open to receiving dreams, visions, or revelation as you read the Bible. It's okay to be vulnerable in God's sight and ask for counsel from those trusted voices in your life.

THE FOOLISH WOMAN

I have always been an independent woman because I was a single mother for many years. Before that, I made a lot of money and didn't depend on anyone to take care of me. When I got remarried, I started a business. A young lady wanted to become a partner, but God spoke through my husband that the answer was no. Then He confirmed it again in a dream. I didn't listen and decided to work with this young lady. She had the wrong spirit upon her and would've taken over my company if I were more passive. I had to repent to the Lord and my husband for not taken heed of their counsel and set boundaries with the young lady. We had a falling out because her motives weren't right. Had I listened, then I wouldn't have gotten hurt in the process.

PRAYER:

Dear Heavenly Father,

You are all-wise and all-knowing. There is none like You. I'm grateful for Your counsel. I bind up any rebellion because that is like the sin of witchcraft. I don't want to rebel against You or the people You sent to warn me. Allow me to

Today's Verse

discern when it's You speaking versus someone who doesn't have my best interest or my flesh telling me what I want to hear. I need You to order my steps and direct my path in life. I truly can't live without You. I am a mess without Your Spirit. I love You and I will do the right thing in life. Thank You for answering this prayer, in Jesus' name. Amen.

DAY 19

Today's Verse

PROVERBS 12:16 SAYS, "A fool's wrath is presently known; but a prudent man covereth shame."

A foolish person won't care if people see them lose control, but a wise man will ignore the insults and walk away. We have to realize that a good name is compared to precious ointment (Ecclesiastes 7:1). When we have an excellent reputation, people will speak highly of us when we aren't around. What we do is a part of our witness for the Lord Jesus Christ. People won't listen, take us seriously, or receive the gospel from us when we act a fool. They will see our hypocritical behavior and say, "If that's what a Christian is like, then I will have no parts of it." You can be angry but don't get out of charac-

Today's Verse

ter because it's not just about you. Lives are depending on us to make it and they need the gifts upon our lives.

When I was going through a divorce, I was very hot-headed. I decide to make my ex-husband's life miserable. I wanted him to pay the price for all the pain he put me through. I went through the ranks on his job and placed complaints against him. I called his commander every day just to expose him because I was upset. I didn't realize how scorned I was and how people labeled me as an angry person. Nothing I did worked because I was actually digging a pit for myself. As a result, the military protected their own soldier and I was seen as an outcast. I was a danger to myself and others but didn't realize it until God showed me how wicked my heart had become. If my ex-husband would've gotten fired from the military, my children would have to suffer and wouldn't receive the benefits they are currently receiving. It took many years for the Lord to restore my reputation and deliver me from all anger and hurt.

PRAYER:

The Foolish Woman

Dear Heavenly Father,

I appreciate You. Thank You for loving me when I am a wreck. You always deliver me and tell me the truth about myself. You know how to soften my heart when it's hard. You know how to comfort me through the pain. You always extend Your kindness when I don't deserve it. Thank You for not allowing me to die in my sin. You set me free and anointed me for Your glory. I am forever grateful for everything. I love You in Jesus' name. Amen.

DAY 20

Today's Verse

Proverbs 12:23 says, "A prudent man concealeth knowledge: but the heart of fools proclaimeth foolishness."

Just because you have a problem or an issue arises doesn't mean that the world should know. Some people can't handle our weaknesses because they have placed us (leaders, five-fold gifts) on pedestals as if we have it all together. Perhaps they start to view us differently when they find out what kind of warfare we encounter. They might lose respect for you when they don't agree with how you handle your problems. Some might even try to curse you or pray that you will stumble. Whatever the case, we have to allow God to restore and fix the broken areas in our lives.

Many people turn to social media when they are going through and they post all their problems. You can learn a lot by going on someone's Facebook page and reading their statuses. They will tell you if they are having marital problems, sick, someone made them mad, who they don't like, who they are dating, and so on. I had people post about me on Facebook. As soon as we disagreed, they posted that I was a false prophet, liar, etc. My flesh wanted to say something, but I knew that is what the enemy wanted, so I didn't even respond to the attacks. I acted like it didn't bother me and decided to use my social media pages for the Lord's glory. I prayed more to receive healing in my heart because I genuinely cared for the person who was attacking me. It's crazy how foolish we look by putting our business on blast. It's like our social media pages are a Lifetime Movie playing for everyone to see. People are grabbing their popcorn and soda for the show. Everyone doesn't need to know everything about you. Let people be proven and tested.

Today's Verse

PRAYER:

Dear Heavenly Father,

I am sorry for the times that I put my business out there for all the world to see. I didn't realize that it was causing a reproach upon You and myself. I now realize that I needed to handle conflict according to Your Word (Matthew 18:15-17). First, I will approach the person in private to resolve any issues. I will wait until I'm in the right spirit to do so. Next, if we can't reach an agreement, then I will have a witness. Lastly, if that fails, then I will bring the matter before the church. You gave us principles in Your Word to follow. I will seek You first and obey Your law in Jesus' name. Amen.

DAY 21

Today's Verse

Proverbs 13:16 says, "Every prudent man dealeth with knowledge: but a fool layeth open his folly."

A wise person has good sense, but a foolish one puts all their stupidity on display. We must realize that we aren't getting any younger. We will be arrested if we fight, destroy property, harass, stalk, or threaten someone, etc. We need to consider the costs and decide that many things are at stake. It's not worth sinning against God or losing our self-control. We must bite our tongues and swallow our pride because someone is looking up to us. It may not feel like it, but someone is inspired by you. Our children, nephews, nieces, grandchildren, great-

Today's Verse

grandchildren, spiritual children, godchildren, siblings, mentees, colleagues, etc., are watching you. We must be a great example and make sure we demonstrate what Jesus would have done in any situation.

Years ago, I was in a heated argument with this lady. She sent my ex-husband naked photos of herself. So I googled her husband, and forwarded all the inappropriate messages to him. She wouldn't stop contacting my ex-husband, so I picked up the phone and cursed her out. My children were smaller, and I acted this way in front of them. I threatened to beat her up and I was about to jump in the car and drive to her house. I planned to put her in the hospital. What would have happened if she would've killed me for being on her property or if I would've gone to jail? I didn't think about that. At the time, my ex-husband was just as guilty as she was, but I didn't realize that until I walked away from the situation. We have to be better examples for our children. It's an oxymoron when you tell your children not to curse or act a fool, but that's all they see you doing. Don't put your family at risk by doing crazy things.

PRAYER:

Dear Heavenly Father,

Help me be a good role model to those that I influence so I can glorify You. I surrender all and I will become so hidden in You that nothing else matters. I have nothing to prove to anyone because they didn't die on the cross for my sins. I know that if I live right and walk uprightly before You, then You will avenge me. You told me in Your Word that vengeance was Yours. I don't want to be petty because life is short. Bless me with the strength to forgive those who wronged me. Thank You for answering this prayer in Jesus' name.

DAY 22

Today's Verse

Proverbs 14:3 says, "In the mouth of the foolish is a rod of pride: but the lips of the wise shall preserve them."

There is an old saying, "Don't put your foot in your mouth." This saying means don't embarrass yourself by saying inappropriate things. How many scandals have happened because someone famous said something racist, sexist, indecent, etc.? Too many to count. A foolish person's mouth will get them in trouble. They are getting involved in useless debates that profit nothing because no solution has been met, no souls are saved, and no one is delivered. The only thing that happened after the heated debate is bruised egos. Some foolish people result in name-calling and form many enemies, which is dangerous. People will kill you over the smallest things or for no reason at all. Don't give the enemy any room. A fool will disrespect those in authority, which is contrary to God's Word. Even if we don't like or agree with those in authority (leaders, President, Vice President, lawyers, judges, policemen, etc.), we still have to honor their position or office.

One day, I wanted to help this lady promote her ministry. God gave me a magazine and a network to promote others. This lady wrote her testimony in her book and I knew someone needed to hear her story. She ended up becoming offended at me because I didn't address her ministry title. She posted about me on her social media networks and she canceled our scheduled meeting. I knew that pride shut the door for her promotion and divine connections that the Lord wanted to bring to her life. Most of everyone that has been on my platform, God has increased the sales of their products, seminars, or supporters. Maybe in another season, God will promote this young lady when she humbles herself.

Today's Verse

PRAYER:

Dear Heavenly Father,

I don't want my mouth to get me in trouble. When I preach your gospel, I don't want my flesh to be seen, but I want people to see Your glory. I refuse to sell out for popularity, fame, or riches. I won't compromise to get people to like me. Season my speech with salt and wisdom so people can be blessed and You will be glorified. Bless me, Lord, to never be caught up in a scandal. I don't want to miss opportunities for divine connections because of pride. Thank You for answering this prayer in Jesus' name. Amen.

DAY 23

Today's Verses

Proverbs 14:16-17 says, "A wise man fearth and departeth from evil: but the fool rageth, and is confident. He that is soon angry dealeth foolishly: and a man of wicked devices is hated."

Things happen in life that will upset us and get us off track. However, we can't allow people to push our buttons. Sometimes when we get angry, we want to yell, throw stuff, hurt people, and lose self-control. We can't do these things because the enemy will try his best to make us go into a rage where we sin against the Lord. Once we cross certain thresholds and boundaries, there is no turning back. Some allow the anger to escalate where they explode to the point that they blackout, murder, or let a host of demonic spirits in. People will hate you if you destroy their lives by allowing anger to rule over your life. For instance, people hate the person who used wicked devices such as guns to murder their loved ones. It takes God to help them forgive that person.

I remember sitting in jail and I had a spirit of murder upon me. I was actually thinking of ways to kill my ex-husband because of what he did to me. I'm so glad that God delivered me right in that jail cell and kept me. For years, I felt like being loud was going to make me more powerful. I loved to argue and cut a person down with my words. I didn't realize that I emasculated my ex-husband at the time. A man needs respect. So after years of disrespect, he didn't want to have anything to do with me. Had I had wisdom, I would've won him over with godly conduct (1 Peter 3:1). We have to love people according to God's Word. We must depart from evil and put our confidence in God. Only He can deliver stubborn people and soften the hardest hearts.

PRAYER:

Dear Heavenly Father,

I bless Your Holy name. I am hurting and I need You to heal my broken heart. I am tired of going through the same old cycles. Please keep me from hurting others and myself. I don't want to be a person who uses wicked devices. I don't want to be argumentative or be a person of drama. I want my home to be peaceful so You can be glorified and Your Spirit can dwell strongly there. I declare that I will depart from evil. I close every demonic portal in my life in Jesus' name. Amen.

DAY 24

Today's Verse

Proverbs 14:33 says, "Wisdom resteth in the heart of him that hath understanding: but that which is in the midst of fools is made known.

Imagine the presence of God resting upon you. Everyone can feel and see it when they cross paths with you. Some may not understand, but they know that there is something different about you. This same concept applies to wisdom and foolishness. The spirit of wisdom can rest upon you that will cause people to seek after your counsel as Queen Sheba did with King Solomon (1 Kings 10). Contrarily a person's folly will be known among everyone like Nabal and his household. Everyone knew Nabal's personality.. He was mean, selfish, and put others in the path of harm (1 Samuel 25).

Out of the abundance of the mouth, the heart speaks (Luke 6:45). When we become upset, we tend to say things that were suppressed. We can't sweep problems under the rug and not deal with them because they will keep coming back up to the surface. When I was battling depression, some important issues weren't resolved, and my husband kept running from them. As a result, I couldn't conceal my feelings any longer and his whole family knew how I felt and the marital problems after we had a public argument. Afterward, the entire family knew our business and some counseled us to walk away from each other instead of praying and encouraging us to fight for the relationship. Not everyone has the best counsel, so we have to be careful who we confide in. We should never fight with our spouses at public gatherings. Marriage is between the Lord, the husband, and the wife.

PRAYER:

Dear Heavenly Father,

Today's Verse

I praise Your Holy name. I apologize for revealing the issues that You have covered. You have always dealt with me privately to get things right. I pray that I will take heed. I don't want to make a mess of the things that You are fixing in my life. I will move out of the way and take my hands off the situation. Thank You, Lord, for Your conviction. I surrender everything to You. I can't do this in my own strength. Lord, I really need You. I trust that Your will is going to be done regardless of what happens. Thank You for answering this prayer in Jesus' name.

DAY 25

Today's Verse

Proverbs 15:2 says, "The tongue of the wise useth knowledge aright: but the mouth of fools poureth out foolishness."

A foolish person has no filter and will say whatever comes to their minds. They don't consider the consequences of their words and care who they hurt or offend. Everything that comes out of their mouth is ignorance. Just because something may be true doesn't mean it needs to be said. For instance, when we minister to someone, we have to say things that will draw people to Christ and not push them further away from Him. There is a way that God will have us deliver a message where people receive it. We have to love people and see God's heart for them.

Today's Verse

When I worked at the hospital, one of my co-workers had a foul mouth. Everything she spoke about was appalling. I truly didn't like her and I heard she had told some of my other co-workers that I needed to hurry up. One co-worker said, "Kim, she is the church," because she saw me read the Bible before. I was backslidden and didn't realize that was a compliment, so I said, "R...better shut the F...up!" I cursed and called out the young lady who I didn't like. Foolishness came out of my mouth and I was a bad representation of Christ and the church. God is gracious that He forgave me for the times I dishonored Him and the church.

PRAYER:

Dear Heavenly Father,

I apologize for tainting what the church is supposed to look like. I am made in Your image and likeness. I am called to be an ambassador of Jesus Christ. Please help me to think about things before I say them. Allow me to speak words in a way that whoever I minister to will receive it. I don't belong to myself. I have been bought with a price when Jesus' shed His blood for me (1 Corinthians 6:20). Purge me Lord, with Hyssop (Psalm 51:7). Create in me a pure heart and renew a steadfast spirit within me (Psalm 51:10). Thank You for answering this prayer in Jesus' name. Amen.

DAY 26

Today's Verse

Proverbs 15:5 says, "A fool despiseth his father's instruction: but he that regardeth reproof is prudent."

God commands us that we honor our mothers and fathers because we will have a long life. Our parents have a level of wisdom that we may not have and more life experiences. If our parents love us, then you should know that they want the best for us. A foolish person hates their parent's instructions. Perhaps they feel like they know everything or no longer want to be submitted to their leadership. If we listen to our parents, we will be spared from heartaches and premature death. Our parents can see the blind spots that we can't see. They can see when someone is a bad influence on their child.

I was a rebellious teen and I dressed provocatively. My father worked at Walmart and he was so embarrassed that his co-workers would be checking me out when I walked into the store half-naked. I didn't listen to him and how it made him feel. My father didn't want any men to take advantage of me because he loved me. He knew that those men were disrespecting me and labeling me as a hoe because that's how I carried myself. My dad was in an awkward situation because he didn't want to lose his job by flipping on these men and he didn't want anyone to talk bad about his daughter. I brought shame upon him. When I saw how much I hurt my father, my heart broke. I apologized and wore more clothes when I went to his job. Years later, the Holy Spirit taught me how to be modest and it was a process.

PRAYER:

Dear Heavenly Father,

Today's Verse

I humble myself. Thank You for placing parents (physical or spiritual) in my life because they love and care about me. If I honor them, then I will have a long life because that is the first commandment with a promise. I realize that my choices affect others. I will keep this in the back of my mind, so I will consider them before doing things. Lord, help me to stay in Your will and mature in You. Bless me to never bring my parent's shame. Thank You for answering this prayer in Jesus' name. Amen.

DAY 27

Today's Verse

Proverbs 17:21 says, "He that begetteth a fool doeth it to his sorrow: and the father of a fool hath no joy."

It's sad being a parent of a fool. How can you have joy when all your foolish child does is bring sorrow? A foolish child goes out of their way to stress their parents out. They make choices that put their family in danger. Parents with foolish children have to believe in God for their deliverance. Parents love to brag about their children and their accomplishments. However, it's difficult to do that with a foolish child. Do you bring your parents joy? Even if your parents are deceased, did you bring them joy?

Today's Verse

I was a runaway child. I gave my parents a lot of grey hairs and sleepless nights. I would rebel against them and when they tried to punish me, I would sneak out of the house and stay away for days at a time. My parents didn't know if I was dead or alive. Sometimes, they felt sick or lost their appetite because of the stress I caused. It took God to save me from the path of destruction to show me how foolish that was for me to run away. As a teenager, I remember telling my mother that I loved her and she would never say it back. It wasn't until I got saved that she started telling me that she loved me.

PRAYER:

Dear Heavenly Father,

I thank You for keeping me even when I was in my ignorance. Thank You for giving me a revelation of the consequences of sin. Lord, break every demonic cycle off me and my bloodline. Bless my children and their children never to make the same mistakes that I have. Keep them from premature death and order their steps. Save my loved ones and deliver my family. Lord, bring restoration to my home. Thank You for answering this prayer in Jesus' name. Amen.

DAY 28

Today's Verse

Proverbs 17:28 says, "Even a fool, when he holdeth his peace, is counted wise: and he that shutteth his lips is esteemed a man of understanding."

A foolish person can look wise when they are quiet. When they keep their lips shut, they appear to understand. Have you ever noticed that the most immature people are the ones that are trying to be seen? They are constantly trying to impress people, but really they don't know much. As soon as the foolish person opens their mouth, they will be exposed and the lack of knowledge will be evident.

THE FOOLISH WOMAN

I remember making up excuses for being cheated on. I had ungodly soul ties and allowed a man to do his dirt then return to me. I would suppress my feelings, but I was hurting on the inside. After I gave my life to the Lord, He showed me my foolishness. I had low self-esteem, but the Lord restored my self-worth. I see many women on social media post a crazy status about being a side chick or having friends with benefits. We have to own our part and stop deceiving ourselves to feel better. If we are broken, then we will attract broken people. Once we are delivered, we will attract other people like ourselves.

PRAYER:

Dear Heavenly Father,

You are wonderful. Show me when to speak and when not to. Bless me with discernment and order my steps. I decree that my body is a slave of righteousness. I don't want to make excuses for my and others shortcomings. I don't want to deceive myself. Bless me with knowledge and godly wisdom. Thank You for Your Word because it's a lamp to my feet and light unto my path. Thank You for answering this prayer in Jesus' name.

DAY 29

Today's Verse

Proverbs 18:7 says, "A fool's mouth is his destruction, and his lips are the snare of his soul."

A foolish person will make false promises, not realizing they are digging themselves into a pit. We have to be people of integrity and keep our vows. Years ago, people could make verbal agreements and honor them. Now the world has become more corrupt and contracts must be written. It's foolish not to have proof of a service. People will take advantage of and manipulate you.

As a teenager, I told this guy that I would date him and pay him a certain amount of money every week if he brought me some timberland boots. I lied and put myself in danger of being raped or jumped by him and his friends. One day, I tricked this boy and got an empty shoebox. I put some Styrofoam inside and called him over. I told him not to look at it until he left. Well, he was upset and threatened to beat me up. I would skip school to avoid him or be late to class because I was afraid. We can't cheat people or wrong them because it could be our destruction.

PRAYER:

Dear Heavenly Father,

I will be a person of integrity and not make false promises. Bless me to do the right thing. I will not compromise and put myself in harm's way by lying and manipulating people. I don't want to spend an eternity in damnation because I sinned against You. I am so grateful that You spared my life because I should've been six feet under. Thank You for Your mercy and grace. I love You. Thanks for answering this prayer, in Jesus' name. Amen.

DAY 30

Today's Verses

Proverbs 19:1,3 says, "Better is the poor that walketh in his integrity, than he that is perverse in his lips, and is a fool. The foolishness of man perverteth his way: and his heart fretteth against the Lord."

Perversion is the twisting of the truth. A fool can deceive themselves by believing in a lie. The enemy or the devil is the master of twisting God's truth and deceiving those who will believe it. The Bible is clear that it's better to be a poor man with integrity than to be a fool, which shows how much God despises foolery. In other words, there is more hope for a poor man because God can bless them financially and bless their life. However, if a fool receives the same financial blessing, they probably will be ruined because they can't handle what God gives them.

It is foolish to become mad at God because He is our help. Most of the time, people are blaming God for their mistakes. God warned them not to connect with people or do certain things, but they didn't listen. However, we have to look in the mirror and own up to our responsibility. When I was going through a divorce, I realized that I had a victim mentality. When I cried out to God, He began to deliver me and deal with me first. I would complain to Him about everyone else. Then He would say, "What about the time you messed up?" I realized that He was right and saw the error of my ways.

PRAYER:

Dear Heavenly Father,

I know that Your Word is the standard that we should live by. I will not twist Your Word to justify sinful actions. Bless me to be a person of integrity, always upholding Your Word. I will not blame You for my mistakes. Bless me to mature

THE FOOLISH WOMAN

and grow up in the knowledge of Your Word. It's foolish to become angry at You because You are a very present help in our time of time. Lord, You are my friend. Thank You for answering this prayer in Jesus' name. Amen.

DAY 31

Today's Verse

Proverbs 20:3 says, "It is an honour for a man to cease from strife: but every fool will be meddling."

Foolish people are always fighting, but when you avoid quarrels, then there is a level of honor that you will walk in. Have you ever witnessed someone picking on people that disagree with them? An example is President Donald Trump. He loves to tweet insults publicly about people who don't have the same point of view. Some people that he attacked are very reputable and have served our country for many years. As a result, some people have been appalled by his actions, and he lost a certain level of honor among many. Some of his allies no longer support him.

THE FOOLISH WOMAN

It's foolish to continue to stir up strife, especially if there is nothing there. We have to put down our agenda and pick up God's. If God can forgive a person, then why can't we? We have messed up numerous times and we want forgiveness? We need to extend the same grace that was given to us. If we continue trying to dig a pit for someone, we will eventually fall into that same pit. There is a law of reciprocity or whatever you sow, you will reap. We have to let go so God can have His way through us.

PRAYER:

Dear Heavenly Father,

I repent for holding grudges and stirring up strife. I declare that I will tell the truth and honor those who paved the way for me. You warn us that You are not mocked so that whatever a man sows He will reap. I chose to forgive because if I don't, You won't forgive my sins. I will not be a vessel of the enemy and cause drama. I bind up scandals and demonic cycles that will try to attach to me. Thank You for answering this prayer in Jesus' name. Amen.

DAY 32

Today's Verse

Proverbs 23:9 says, "Speak not in the ears of a fool: for he will despise the wisdom of thy words."

Have you ever tried to warn someone, but they refused to listen? Perhaps, God gave you word for them or you saw the potential disaster that was waiting to happen. Well, you did your part so that blood will not be on your hands. Unfortunately, many people wish they would've listened when they got in trouble, sick, or in worse situations. God does speak through people, but we must discern who and have an ear to hear. It's foolish to despise words of wisdom because tomorrow isn't promised to anyone. Some things are life and death. If you chose foolishly, then you might as well pick out your burial plot and casket.

I have encountered many people in ministry who wanted to waste my time. They didn't want to hear the counsel that God gave me for them. Instead, they wanted me to listen and agree with their erroneous ways. I realized that these types of people are a distraction, and if I allowed them to take up all my time, then I can't do what God is calling me to do. My schedule is very busy and I can't be on the phone with someone for four hours. One day, this lady begged me to call her, so I did, but she didn't want anything important. She wanted to be my best friend, which doesn't happen overnight. That position is earned over time. I ignored her calls and she got the point. Some people are leeches and will drain you. Afterward, you are heavy, tired, and don't even feel like doing Your God given assignment. It's foolish to allow people to waste your time.

PRAYER:

Dear Heavenly Father,

Today's Verse

I praise Your Holy name. Bless me to be a great steward over my time. I don't want to procrastinate and delay what You are telling me to do. I bind up distractions. Bless me with boldness so I can tell people, "No. Not right now. I can't. etc." I will set my face like a flint and will not take it personal if someone rejects the message that You gave me for them. Also, I will not despise prophecy or warnings that You send people to give me. Help me to discern spiritual leeches or people sent by Satan to derail me from my purpose. Lord, You have my full permission to remove anyone out of my life that doesn't need to be there. Thank You for answering this prayer in Jesus' name. Amen.

DAY 33

Today's Verse

Proverbs 26:4 says, "Answer not a fool according to his folly, lest thou also be like unto him."

If we answer foolish people according to their folly, silliness, or erroneous ways, we are no different from them. We are just as foolish. If someone gets an attitude, should we get one back? If someone rolls their eyes, should you roll your eyes as well? If someone just started cursing you out, should you curse back? If someone stole something from you, should you steal because it happened to you? The enemy wants you to respond foolishly so you can sin against God. He loves to see you wreck your life because his job is to kill, steal, and destroy.

Today's Verse

When people attack me on social media, I don't attack back because I know that I must uphold the standard of the Lord as a leader. God gave me influence and responsibility that most don't have, so I must be a great steward over what has been imparted. I never asked for a position or title, but I realize that what I do will impact many people. One day, someone was extremely rude to me. They wanted to argue and accused me of hate crimes because I posted a Scripture that convicted them of their sinful lifestyle. I just loved them and replied respectfully. That person apologized to me shortly afterward because they felt bad for treating me badly when I was very kind. We can't give in to a fool's folly because we won't win anyone to the Lord Christ Jesus.

PRAYER:

Dear Heavenly Father,

Place Your love in my heart so I can love people regardless if they are kind to me. I will be patient and compassionate because many are

THE FOOLISH WOMAN

lost and need a Savior. Allow me to know how to witness to them so they can accept Jesus Christ into their hearts. I don't want to lead people astray because I acted foolishly. I want to respond the way Jesus would in every situation. I put down my pride and any agendas. I just want to do Your will and make You happy. Thank You for answering this prayer in Jesus' name. Amen.

DAY 34

Today's Verse

Proverbs 26:11 says, "As a dog returneth to his vomit, so a fool returneth to his folly."

There is a saying that you can't teach an old dog new tricks because they have been trained to do certain things and won't stray from their routine. A dog will eat something that made them sick then vomit. Afterward, they will lick it back up again. That's how it is with a fool. They know something is wrong but can't stop doing it. They know that they are killing themselves or jeopardizing their freedom, but they are in too deep or love the thrill. A fool will return to danger or a toxic environment regardless of the warning that they received.

THE FOOLISH WOMAN

I went through a season where it seemed like every spirit that I got delivered from came back to attack me with a vengeance. I had to fast and pray so I wouldn't sin. I submitted to God, resisted the devil, and he fled. I passed every test except for one: the anger test. I had allowed one of my family members to get me in my flesh. As a result, I ended up back at square one and all the process that I made over the years was gone. I was devastated and prayed for another chance to get it right. The Holy Spirit took me to the Bible and my eyes fell upon Proverbs 26:11. Conviction sat in and I constantly think about this verse to help me stay on track.

PRAYER:

Dear Heavenly Father,

I bind up the spirit of sabotage and self-destruction, in Jesus' name. I don't want to return to the thing that You have delivered me from. I have come a long way and I refuse to go backward. Please help me to get it right so I can learn from my mistakes. Shield me from demonic attacks because I don't want to lose what You

Today's Verse

blessed me with. I forgive myself for acting foolish. I surrender everything to You, Lord. I will walk uprightly before You. I declare that I will pass every test in Jesus' name. Amen.

DAY 35

Today's Verse

Ecclesiastes 7:9 says, "Be not hasty in thy spirit to be angry: for anger resteth in the bosom of fools."

Don't be quick to anger or be hasty. We can't be hot-tempered because it will destroy our lives. Many people go from zero to one hundred in a few seconds. They just explode in anger and ruin everything in their path. Anger lodges in the bosoms of fools. Foolish people allow this spirit to consume them and run their lives. They don't gather all the facts. They make assumptions and just react without thinking things through. As a result, many people are hurt by their foolery.

Today's Verse

I was quick-tempered and I could feel myself getting hot inside when I became upset. My tone changed and I grew very confrontational. I would assume the worst and felt like everyone was my enemy. I would attack the very people who loved me. I remember sitting in jail, and I read Ecclesiastes 7:9 for the first time. It felt like a ton of bricks hit me. I couldn't believe that I was considered a fool because I thought I had it all together. This verse brought deliverance and healing to my life when I went through a horrible divorce. I meditated on it and got set free.

PRAYER:

Dear Heavenly Father,

I praise You Lord. Bless me not to be hasty and make assumptions. I surrender all my flaws and insecurities unto You so You can do a mighty work within me. I don't want to carry all the hurt and pain any longer. Lord, heal my heart and soul. Purify me with Your fire. Let Your love rest upon me. Allow me to demonstrate Your love to others and pray for them even if they are at fault. I chose to forgive and let go. I will seek

You always for Your counsel. Thank You for answering this prayer in Jesus' name. Amen.

DAY 36

Today's Verse

Ecclesiastes 7:17 says, 'Be not over much wicked, neither be thou foolish: why shouldest thou die before thy time?"

A lot of people have died prematurely due to foolish mistakes. They opened a portal to the enemy. As a result, their life was cut short. God gave us His Word as instructions on how to live. If we are outside of His will, He can't protect us. Sin equals death and gives the enemy access. No one gets away with doing evil. It eventually catches up to them, and they will suffer in this life or eternity. The next time you do something crazy, pause and ask, "If I do this, then what are the consequences? Will I lose my life? Will my soul burn in hell?" Sin isn't worth it. Trust the Lord to fight your battles.

I had a middle school friend who got connected to the wrong crowd. She started liking females and she wanted me. I turned her down and separated myself. Even though I was living a fast lifestyle, she did things that I didn't do, such as crack, ecstasy, heroin, and sold drugs. We stopped talking. Several years later, I ran into her cousin, a nurse, when I worked in the hospital. She asked me, "Hey did you know F..?" I said, "Yes." "Well, she died. She was high on drugs and walked into oncoming traffic," the nurse replied. When I heard the news of her death, I was shocked. I knew it was the devil that took her out because demons can enter people through drugs. My friend had a lot of potential and died without ever fulfilling her purpose.

PRAYER:

Dear Heavenly Father,

I am so grateful that You protected me when I was living foolishly in the world. I am here for

Today's Verse

a reason, which is to bring You glory. Help me God, to use wisdom, so the promise of a long life will be fulfilled. You have so many awesome plans for my life, and I want to experience them. Draw me closer to You God, so I can follow after You. Many people have died prematurely, and that could've been me. I am blessed and favored by You. I will not take that for granted. Thank You, God for everything in Jesus' name. Amen.

DAY 37

Today's Verses

GALATIANS 3:1,3 SAYS, "O foolish Galatians, who hath bewitched you, that ye should not obey the truth, before whose eyes Jesus Christ hath been evidently set forth, crucified among you?...Are ye so foolish? Having begun in the Spirit, are ye now made perfect by the flesh?"

Some people are bewitched and following false ministers, which is a very foolish thing because they follow them straight to hell. The beast and false prophets will be in the lake of fire (Revelation 20:10). They will feel the wrath of God. We must choose God over man even if someone is our favorite preacher, has a great personality, or good looking. If a person is not preaching the Bible or Jesus, run because you will get sucked into the spirit of seduction upon their lives. It will be harder to come out of bondage then because you will be bewitched, and they can indoctrinate you with falsehoods.

Throughout church history, there have been many that have risen with the Messiah complex. They made themselves gods in people's lives. Some have even confessed that they were Jesus in the flesh, the second Elijah, or the face-to-face prophet, and their followers believed it. These false teachers weren't living holy. They want glory, fame, riches, sex, power, etc. I have seen many cults on social media where people call these false ministers, lord of lords, king of kings, and changed their last name to the same as the wicked leader, which is foolery. One day, these people will have a rude awakening on Judgement day. They will stand before Jesus and hear the words, "Depart from me, you workers of iniquity. I never knew you."

PRAYER:

Dear Heavenly Father,

THE FOOLISH WOMAN

Bless me to get deeper into Your Word, so I can know the truth. Your Spirit is life and truth. I don't want to be deceived or bamboozled by the enemy. I don't want to follow anyone to hell because I can't see their wickedness or lack discernment. Warn me, Holy Spirit, that something isn't right. Don't let me be led astray. Don't ever allow me to be a part of a cult. If I am, bless me to cut all ties. Break demonic soul ties off my life. Break every word curse in the name of Jesus. Amen.

DAY 38

Today's Verse

Ephesians 5:15 says, "See then that ye walk circumspectly, not as fools, but as wise."

We have to be careful how we live because it's not only about us. If you have God's hand upon your life, then you will realize that you are called to serve others with the anointing you carry. Even when you don't feel like ministering, there will be a great demand for it. Ministry never stops because people are lost, broken, sick, bound, weary, hopeless, etc. We can't do what the world is doing. Why do you want to be carnal? Why do you want to blend in with the world? Why do you hide the fact that you are saved? Are you ashamed of Jesus? We must practice the Word of God by walking it out.

THE FOOLISH WOMAN

There was a prophet on social media who walked foolishly. He lost his credibility when multiple scandals came out against him. There was evidence, so there was no denying the facts. He had lied many times, had sex with multiple women, and got involved in divination. His ministry was at the top of the pinnacle. Now, his ministry isn't the same. His view count dropped by several thousand and the size of his meets decreased drastically. It was sad to see doors slam in his face. We have to live holy and put forth the sacrifice that it takes to keep our salvation. If you suffered for the anointing, then why lose it by doing crazy things?

PRAYER:

Dear Heavenly Father,

You are precious and the best thing that has ever happened to me. I don't want to take You for granted nor the gifts and talents upon my life. I am a bondservant for Christ. I will walk circumspectly by placing boundaries and safeguards, so I don't sin against You. Lord, remove

Today's Verse

every demonic stumble block before me. Lord, you are my confidence and will keep my feet from being caught. Thank You for answering this prayer in Jesus' name. Amen.

About The Author

KIMBERLY MOSES STARTED OFF her ministry as Kimberly Hargraves. She is highly sought after as a prophetic voice, intercessor and prolific author. There is no doubt that she has a global mandate on her life to serve the nations of the world by spreading the Gospel of Jesus Christ. She has a quickly expanding worldwide healing and deliverance ministry. Kimberly Moses wears many hats to fulfill the call God has placed on her life as an entrepreneur over several businesses including her own personal brand Rejoice Essentials which promotes the Gospel of Jesus Christ.

She also serves as a life coach and mentor to many women. She is also the loving mother of

About The Author

two wonderful children. She is married to Tron. Kimberly has dedicated her life to the work of ministry and to serve others under the call God has placed over her life. Kimberly currently resides in South Carolina.

She is a very anointed woman of God who signs, miracles and wonders follow. The miraculous and incessant testimonies attributed to her ministry are incalculable, with many reporting physical and mental healing, financial breakthroughs, debt cancellations and other favorable outcomes. She is known across the globe as a servant who truly labors on behalf of God's people through intercession.

She is the author of The Following:

"Overcoming Difficult Life Experiences with Scriptures and Prayers"
"Overcoming Emotions with Prayers"
"Daily Prayers That Bring Changes"
"In Right Standing,"
"Obedience Is Key,"
"Prayers That Break The Yoke Of The Enemy: A Book Of Declarations,"

"Prayers That Demolish Demonic Strongholds: A Book Of Declarations,"

"Work Smarter. Not Harder. A Book Of Declarations For The Workforce,"

"Set The Captives Free: A Book Of Deliverance."

"Pray More Challenge"

"Walk By Faith: A Daily Devotional"

"Empowering The New Me: Fifty Tips To Becoming A Godly Woman"

"School of the Prophets: A Curriculum For Success"

"8 Keys To Accessing The Supernatural"

"Conquering The Mind: A Daily Devotional"

"Enhancing The Prophetic In You"

"The ABCs of The Prophetic: Prophetic Characteristics"

"Wisdom Is The Principal Thing: A Daily Devotional"

"It Cost Me Everything"

"The Making Of A Prophet: Women Walking in Prophetic Destiny"

"The Art of Meditation: A Daily Devotional"

"Warfare Strategies: Biblical Weapons"

"Becoming A Better You"

"I Almost Died"

"The Pastor's Secret: The D.L. Series"

About The Author

"June Bug The Busy Bee: The Gamer"
"June Bug The Busy Bee: The Bully"
"The Weary Prophet: Providing Practical Steps For Restoration"
"The Insignificant Woman"

You can find more about Kimberly at www.kimberlyhargraves.com

For Rejoice Essential Magazine, visit www.rejoiceessential.com

For beauty and t-shirts, visit www.rejoicingbeauty.com

Please write a review for my books on Amazon.com

Support this ministry:
Cashapp: $ProphetessKimberly
Paypal.me/remag
Venmo: Kimberly-Moses-19

Index

A

abominable works, 28
abundance, 24, 88
accelerated, 52
access, 11, 121
accomplishments, 96
account, 64
actions, 3, 6, 11, 14, 37, 49, 105, 107
advantage, 94, 102
advice, 24
afflicted, 11, 42, 43
afflictions, 42
afraid, 19, 45, 103
agenda, 108
agents of Satan, 11

Index

alcohol, 42, 52
alignment, 47
ambassador, 91
anger, 2, 4, 5, 16, 52, 55, 73, 84, 85, 116, 118
Anger, 1, 18, 118
angry, 57, 58, 72, 73, 84, 106, 118
animal, 39
annoyed, 49
anointing, 127, 128
apologized, 94, 113
appalling, 91
appetite, 97
argue, 29, 85, 113
argument, 79, 88
argumentative, 86
arrest, 61
arrested, 32, 55, 78
arrogant, 25
Asaph, 39
ashamed, 127
assignment, 37, 110
assumptions, 118, 119
astray, 114, 126
attacked, 26, 107
attacking, 76
attorneys, 3

attract, 100
author, 131
authority, 82
avenge, 16, 56, 80
avoid, 61, 103, 107

B

backslidden, 38, 91
backslide, 43
bail, 2, 3
bail bonds agents, 2
bait, 9, 23
bamboozled, 18, 126
bank, 4
banned, 55
battle, 19
beast, 39, 124
beat, 79, 103
beautiful, 61
believe, 1, 2, 96, 104, 119
belly, 2
beneficial, 46
benefits, 73, 100
bewitch, 18
bewitched, 124, 125

Index

Bible, 6, 52, 69, 91, 104, 116, 124
bills, 3, 64
birds, 40
bitterness, 4
black woman, 58
Black women, 57
blackout, 84
blame, 105
blasphemy, 29
Bless, 9, 10, 35, 53, 65, 80, 83, 95, 97, 100, 103, 105, 111, 119, 126
blessed, 3, 26, 83, 117, 123
blessedness, 28
blood, 56, 92, 109
bloodline, 97
blurt, 23
boastful, 25
bodies, 5, 42, 43
boils, 23
bondage, 125
bondservant, 128
book, 2, 6, 82
books, 6, 63, 133
boots, 103
bosom, 18, 118
bother, 76

bound, 5, 127
boundaries, 70, 84, 128
broken, 76, 86, 100, 127
broken heart, 86
broken people, 100
build, 4, 7, 46, 51
burdens, 35
bushes, 19
business, 10, 15, 50, 58, 63, 69, 70, 76, 77, 88
busy, 110
Busy Bee, 133

C

Captives, 132
car, 79
careless, 11
carnal, 127
cast out, 5
category, 58
caves, 19
Celebrities, 39
cervical cancer, 43
cervix, 43
chair, 55
Challenges, 69

chaos, 22
character, 3, 32
Characteristics, 132
chastise, 64
cheated, 100
cheaters, 58
children, 16, 22, 28, 34, 42, 73, 78, 79, 96, 97, 131
choices, 3, 7, 52, 95, 96
Christ, 13, 18, 54, 62, 72, 90, 91, 113, 114, 124, 128, 130
Christian, 1, 49, 72
church, 52, 56, 77, 91, 125
circles, 57
circumspectly, 18, 127, 128
circumstances, 59
cirrhosis, 42
clamorous, 13, 57, 59
clothes, 94
collaboration, 48
colleagues, 79
comfort, 26, 74
commander, 73
commandment, 19, 95
commandments, 8, 60
community service, 67

compare, 39, 40

compassion, 14

compassionate, 113

complaining, 40

complaints, 73

complement, 6

compromise, 62, 83, 103

confess, 4, 29

confidence, 85, 129

confident, 84

conflict, 77

confront, 67

confrontational, 55, 119

consequences, 3, 6, 14, 32, 49, 90, 97, 121

consume, 16, 38, 118

contracts, 102

control, 49, 72, 78, 84

convicted, 113

Conviction, 116

cops, 58, 60

correctional officer, 2

corrupt, 28, 102

costs, 78

counsel, 12, 15, 23, 24, 46, 47, 50, 53, 69, 70, 87, 88, 110, 120

counseling, 49

Index

court case, 3
court costs, 3
cousin, 122
co-workers, 55, 91, 94
crack, 122
crazy things, 6, 79, 128
Creator, 28, 45
creatures, 28, 40
credibility, 128
criminal charges, 52
cross, 43, 80, 84, 87
cry, 1, 4
cult, 18, 126
Curriculum, 132
curse, 22, 26, 49, 75, 79, 112, 126
cursed, 23, 79, 91
cursing, 23, 112
cycle, 57, 97
cycles, 6, 8, 33, 59, 86, 108

D

damnation, 103
danger, 28, 42, 73, 96, 103, 115
dangerous, 42, 49, 66, 82
date, 102

dating, 76
daughter, 94
David, 25, 26, 31
death, 17, 34, 42, 43, 109, 121, 122
debates, 81
debt cancellations, 131
debts, 4
deceased, 96
deceive, 100, 104
deceived, 126
decisions, 50, 51
Declarations, 131, 132
decree, 7, 11, 27, 100
defended, 67
delay, 20, 111
delayed, 20
delights, 26
deliver, 31, 33, 73, 74, 85, 90, 97, 105
Deliver, 10, 31, 38, 59
deliverance, 4, 5, 6, 7, 96, 119, 130
deliverance process, 4
delivered, 4, 32, 38, 81, 85, 100, 116
delusional, 29
demon, 5
demonic portal, 86
demonic stronghold, 33

Index

demons, 122

demonstrates, 68

demoted, 12, 52

demotion, 53

deny, 9, 12, 29, 30

denying, 128

depart, 16, 85, 86

depressed., 49

deserve, 38, 58, 74

despise, 9, 12, 16, 45, 109, 111

despises, 104

destroy, 4, 23, 78, 85, 112, 118

destruction, 39, 40, 63, 97, 102, 103, 116

Destruction, 14

determination, 32

devastated, 116

devastating, 3

devices, 16, 84, 85, 86

devil, 4, 8, 23, 24, 66, 104, 116, 122

devotional, 6

Devotional, 132

devout, 22

die, 34, 43, 74, 80, 121

dirt, 100

disagreed, 76

disagreement, 17

disappointed, 58
disaster, 109
disbelief, 1
discern, 48, 71, 109, 111
discernment, 11, 15, 51, 100, 126
discouraged, 40
disgrace, 13
dishonor, 4
dishonored, 91
disobedient, 50
disrespect, 82, 85
distance, 9
distraction, 110
divination, 128
divine connections, 82, 83
divorce, 32, 73, 105, 119
dog, 17, 115
dogs, 58
dollars, 64
domestic violence, 3
dominion, 40
Donald Trump, 107
double portion, 53
download, 2
drain, 110
drama, 15, 86, 108

dream, 28, 70
dreams, 69
drugs, 40, 42, 122
dry place, 5
due season, 27
dwell, 5, 25, 86

E

ear to hear, 53, 109
ecstasy, 122
ego, 16
egos, 81
Elijah, 125
emasculated, 85
embarrass, 81
embarrassed, 64, 94
embarrassment, 3, 33
emotions, 39, 49
Empowering, 132
encountered, 110
enemies, 26, 31, 32, 33, 82
enemy, 4, 9, 18, 23, 26, 38, 68, 76, 82, 84, 104, 108, 112, 119, 121, 126
energy, 17
entrepreneur, 130

environments, 12
erroneous ways, 110, 112
error, 105
eternal damnation, 29
eternity, 39, 103, 121
evidence, 128
evident, 51, 99
evil, 16, 18, 22, 54, 84, 85, 86, 121
excuses, 100
ex-husband, 4, 73, 79, 85
exotic dancer, 61
expenses, 3, 64
expensive, 3
expose, 73
exposed, 31, 66, 99
eyes, 15, 69, 112, 116, 124

F

face, 2, 22, 55, 67, 69, 111, 125, 128
Facebook page, 76
faith, 2, 20
faithful, 40, 64
false ministers, 124, 125
falsehoods, 125
fame, 83, 125

Index

family, 2, 4, 5, 10, 35, 38, 58, 69, 79, 88, 96, 97, 116
famous, 40, 81
fast, 49, 116, 122
fault, 4, 119
favor, 51, 53, 68
favorable outcomes, 131
favorite preacher, 124
fear, 45
feelings, 40, 88, 100
feet, 62, 103, 129
fellowshipping, 40
fighting, 1, 35, 56, 107
finances, 10, 51
financial breakthroughs, 131
financially, 104
flashbacks, 1
flaws, 119
flesh, 56, 71, 76, 83, 116, 124, 125
folly, 17, 18, 78, 87, 112, 113, 115
food, 64
fool, 17, 28, 34, 60, 66, 69, 72, 78, 79, 82, 84, 93, 96, 99, 102, 104, 107, 109, 112, 113, 115, 119
foolery, 7, 11, 38, 104, 118, 125
foolish, 4, 6, 9, 10, 11, 12, 13, 15, 17, 20, 21, 22, 23, 24, 25, 29, 31, 32, 33, 34, 35, 37, 38, 39, 43,

50, 51, 54, 55, 56, 57, 60, 63, 66, 72, 76, 78, 81, 90, 93, 96, 97, 99, 102, 105, 106, 108, 109, 110, 112, 117, 121, 124

Foolish, 3, 42, 107, 118

foolish child, 96

foolish things, 6, 43, 56

foolish woman, 4, 6, 23, 24, 57

foolishly, 2, 3, 8, 19, 27, 39, 84, 109, 112, 114, 122, 128

foolishness, 11, 14, 15, 37, 75, 87, 90, 100, 104

Foolishness, 57, 91

fools, 45, 48, 51, 75, 87, 90, 118, 127

foot, 81

forfeited, 20

forgave, 91

forgive, 1, 15, 50, 80, 85, 108, 117, 119

forgiven, 2

forgiveness, 4, 108

Forsake, 54

forsook, 55

free, 1, 33, 59, 74, 119

freedom, 115

fret, 17

friend, 67, 106, 110, 122

fulfilling, 122

furious, 55, 67

Index

G

game, 14, 48
gas money, 64
generation, 5
George Floyd, 58
ghetto, 57
gifts, 73, 75, 128
glorified, 83, 86
glorify, 36, 80
glory, 29, 38, 51, 53, 74, 76, 83, 123, 125
God, 1, 3, 4, 6, 8, 9, 10, 12, 19, 20, 22, 23, 25, 26, 28, 29, 31, 37, 38, 39, 40, 45, 46, 48, 49, 51, 52, 54, 55, 58, 59, 61, 63, 64, 66, 67, 69, 70, 73, 76, 78, 82, 85, 87, 90, 91, 93, 96, 97, 104, 105, 108, 109, 110, 112, 113, 116, 121, 123, 124, 127, 130,131
godchildren, 79
Godly Woman, 132
good looking, 124
good sense, 78
good steward, 7, 50
gospel, 72, 83
Gospel of Jesus Christ, 29, 130
gossip, 56, 66, 68

gossiping, 55

grace, 53, 61, 103, 108

gracious, 64, 91

grandchildren, 78, 79

grateful, 70, 74, 103, 122

grey hairs, 97

grieve, 8, 11, 27, 45, 56

grieved, 3, 58

growth, 10, 45, 63

grudges, 108

guidance, 53

guilty, 79

gun violence, 42

guns, 85

gynecologist, 43

H

half-naked, 94

hallway, 55

hands, 2, 4, 20, 21, 33, 56, 89, 109

happy, 4, 39, 60, 114

harass, 78

harm, 29, 57, 88, 103

hasty, 9, 118, 119

hate, 9, 24, 45, 48, 68, 85, 113

hated, 26, 67, 84
hates, 25, 66, 93
heal, 86, 119
healing, 6, 76, 119, 130, 131
hearer, 61
hearken, 15
heart attacks, 42
heartache,, 46
heartaches, 93
hearts, 4, 29, 37, 45, 85, 114
Heavenly Father, 21, 24, 26, 29, 32, 35, 38, 40, 43, 46, 50, 53, 55, 59, 61, 64, 68, 70, 74, 77, 80, 83, 86, 88, 91, 94, 97, 100, 103, 105, 108, 110, 113, 116, 119, 122, 125, 128
hell, 18, 122, 124, 126
help, 1, 2, 3, 6, 12, 46, 64, 82, 85, 91, 95, 105, 106, 116
Hepatitis, 42
heroin, 122
herpes, 43
hidden, 54, 80
hindrance, 10
history, 35, 125
HIV, 42
Holiness, 25
holy, 27, 125, 128

Holy Spirit, 5, 21, 29, 45, 54, 94, 116, 126
honest, 14
honor, 16, 53, 82, 93, 95, 102, 107, 108
hope, 104
hopeless, 127
hopes, 29
hospital, 55, 79, 91, 122
hosts of wickedness, 56
hot-tempered, 118
house, 4, 5, 7, 38, 52, 67, 79, 97
household, 87
humans, 40
humble, 12, 21, 27, 33, 46, 50, 64, 65, 95
humbled, 1
humbles, 82
humiliating, 67
hurt, 4, 32, 70, 73, 84, 90, 94, 118, 119
hurting, 2, 86, 100
husband, 43, 52, 70, 73, 79, 85, 88
hustler, 61
hypocrite, 38
hypocritical behavior, 72

I

idol, 52

Index

ignorance, 90, 97
ignorant, 11, 39, 57
image, 91
immature ones, 48
impact, 113
imparted, 113
impatience, 8
impatient, 19, 20, 21
impress, 99
inappropriate messages, 79
inappropriate things, 81
independent woman, 70
indoctrinate, 125
influence, 80, 94, 113
information, 66
inherit, 51, 59
inheritance, 10, 34, 35
insecurities, 68, 119
insight, 12
Insignificant Woman, 133
inspired, 78
instruction, 12, 16, 45, 93
instructions, 45, 60, 93, 121
insults, 72, 107
insurance, 35
integrity, 15, 102, 103, 104, 105

intelligent, 40
intercessor, 130
interest, 71
Iodine, 43
Israel, 19
issue, 75

J

jail, 1, 3, 30, 79, 85, 119
jail cell, 85
jealous, 39
jealousy, 68
jeopardizing, 115
Jesus, 2, 7, 8, 18, 21, 24, 26, 27, 29, 30, 33, 36, 38, 40, 41, 43, 44, 47, 50, 53, 56, 59, 62, 65, 68, 71, 72, 74, 77, 79, 80, 83, 86, 89, 91, 92, 95, 98, 101, 103, 106, 108, 111, 113, 114, 116, 117, 120, 123, 124, 125, 126, 127, 129, 130
jobs, 57
journey, 46
joy, 26, 96
Judgement day, 125
judges, 82
judgment, 23, 45, 64
justify, 105

K

kids, 1, 38
kill, 56, 82, 85, 112
killed, 60, 79
Kimberly, 130, 131, 133
kind, 38, 75, 113
king of kings, 125
kingdom, 19, 20
knowledge, 14, 45, 48, 63, 65, 75, 78, 90, 99, 100, 106
knowledgeable, 49

L

lake of fire, 124
lamp to my feet, 101
last will, 35
law, 77, 108
lawyers, 82
lazy, 63
leaders, 46, 75, 82
leadership, 16, 93
learn, 46, 48, 63, 65, 76, 116
learning, 13, 49, 63

leeches, 110, 111
legacy, 36
legal battles, 35
leisure time, 48
lesson, 65
lessons, 46
license, 55
lie, 66, 104
lied, 103, 128
life, 2, 7, 11, 12, 14, 17, 20, 21, 22, 23, 28, 32, 33, 34, 35, 37, 38, 39, 40, 41, 43, 46, 48, 49, 50, 51, 52, 53, 65, 69, 71, 73, 80, 82, 84, 85, 86, 89, 93, 95, 100, 103, 104, 109, 111, 112, 119, 121, 123, 126, 127, 128, 130, 131
light, 2, 37, 51, 101
lilies of the field, 40
lips, 8, 14, 17, 22, 40, 66, 81, 99, 102, 104
listen, 70, 72, 93, 94, 105, 109, 110
livestock, 22
long life, 95
looters, 58
looting, 58
Lord, 1, 2, 3, 4, 5, 6, 7, 8, 9, 10, 11, 12, 13, 15, 16, 17, 20, 21, 23, 24, 25, 26, 31, 32, 33, 36, 37, 39, 40, 43, 45, 49, 51, 53, 54, 59, 62, 70, 72, 73, 76,

82, 83, 84, 88, 89, 92, 95, 97, 100, 104, 106, 111, 113, 117, 119, 122, 128, 129
lord of lords, 125
lost, 20, 32, 55, 97, 107, 114, 127, 128
love, 9, 15, 24, 25, 37, 48, 53, 61, 68, 71, 74, 85, 90, 93, 95, 96, 103, 113, 115, 119
loved, 13, 22, 35, 85, 94, 97, 113, 119
loving, 64, 74, 130
low self-esteem, 100
lust of the flesh, 14
lying, 14, 29, 66, 103

M

mad, 76, 105
magazine, 82
manifest, 41
manipulate, 102
marital problems, 76, 88
marriage, 32, 38, 43, 52
Marriage, 88
marriages, 10, 39
mature, 50, 95, 105
mean, 24, 54, 57, 59, 75, 88, 90
mean spirited, 57
meddling, 17, 107

medical doctor, 32
Meditation, 132
meeting, 48, 82
memory, 35
mental institution, 30
mentees, 79
mentor, 130
mentors, 46
merciful, 31
mercy, 3, 31, 53, 103
mess up, 4
message, 28, 90, 111
messed up, 1, 20, 105, 108
mind, 1, 18, 23, 49, 55, 95
minds, 29, 48, 90
minister, 1, 29, 30, 32, 90, 91
ministering, 127
ministry, 1, 2, 10, 26, 69, 82, 110, 128, 130, 131, 133
mirror, 4, 105
miserable, 73
mistakes, 11, 32, 42, 51, 97, 105, 116, 121
mocked, 108
modest, 94
Monday, 37
money, 4, 34, 38, 64, 70, 102

moon, 28
motives, 20, 21, 38, 70
mountain, 18
mountains, 28
mouth, 8, 16, 23, 24, 63, 81, 83, 88, 90, 91, 99, 102
murder, 42, 84, 85

N

naïve, 14
name-calling, 81
narrow path, 13, 62
nations, 130
nephews, 78
network, 82
nieces, 78
noisy, 57
noncompliant, 61
numb, 1
nurse, 122

O

Obedience, 131
obedient, 12

obey, 77, 124
oceans, 28
offended, 50, 82
offenses, 15, 68
offering, 19
office, 82
ointment, 72
omnipresent, 25
opinions, 45, 58
opportunities, 50, 83
order, 5, 7, 20, 43, 53, 61, 71, 97, 100
organ failure, 42
outcast, 73
Overcoming, 131
overwhelmed, 1
oxymoron, 79

P

pain, 46, 73, 74, 119
painful, 23
panic, 49
pap-smear, 43
parents, 16, 93, 95, 96, 97
Parents, 96
paring knife, 67

patient, 20, 113
paved, 108
pay, 3, 52, 58, 73, 102
peace, 16, 40, 99
peaceful, 86
perish, 34, 39
permission, 22, 111
persecution, 25
personality, 124
perversion, 17
Perversion, 104
petty, 80
Philistines, 19
phone, 2, 3, 79, 110
phone call, 2
phone numbers, 2
phony, 68
photos, 79
pinnacle, 128
pit, 14, 60, 73, 102, 108
plans, 18, 49, 55, 123
planted, 29
platform, 58, 82
pleasing, 21, 38, 40, 68
pleasure, 26
police, 58, 60

policemen, 82
political matters, 58
poor decisions, 20, 43
poor man, 104
popcorn, 76
popular, 40, 54
Popularity, 54
portal, 121
position, 82, 110, 113
powerful, 59, 85
powers, 56
practice, 55, 127
praise, 40, 58, 89, 111, 119
prating fool, 13, 60, 61
pray, 21, 31, 46, 50, 52, 65, 66, 68, 75, 89, 116, 119
prayer, 1, 21, 25, 27, 30, 38, 41, 44, 47, 50, 53, 56, 59, 62, 65, 68, 71, 80, 83, 89, 92, 95, 98, 101, 103, 106, 108, 111, 114, 120, 129
PRAYER, 32, 35, 38, 40, 43, 46, 50, 52, 55, 59, 61, 64, 67, 70, 73, 77, 80, 83, 85, 88, 91, 94, 97, 100, 103, 105, 108, 110, 113, 116, 119, 122, 125, 128
prayers, 6
Prayers, 7, 131, 132
preach, 29, 83

Index

premature death, 11, 93, 97

preparations, 35

presence, 25, 26, 27, 29, 45, 87

preserve, 51, 81

President, 82, 107

price, 73, 92

pride, 4, 5, 16, 27, 46, 54, 56, 65, 78, 81, 82, 83, 114

prideful, 64

priest, 20

Prince of Peace, 40

principalities, 56

principles, 77

priorities, 35

problem, 75

problems, 55, 75, 76, 88

proclaim, 15

procrastinate, 111

procrastinating, 50

products, 82

profit, 81

prolific author, 130

promiscuous lifestyle, 43

promised, 109

promises, 8, 21, 41, 59, 61, 102, 103

promote, 51, 82

promotion, 51, 53, 82
proof, 102
property, 4, 52, 78, 79
prophet, 1, 76, 125, 128
prophetic, 130
prospering, 39
protected, 26, 30, 73, 122
protection, 53, 61
protests, 58
proud, 50
prove, 54, 55, 56, 80
proven, 76
provision, 53
prudent, 72, 75, 78, 93
publishing business, 63
punish, 97
pure, 8, 21, 24, 37, 92
pure heart, 8, 92
purge, 9
Purify, 33, 119

Q

Queen Sheba, 87
quick-tempered, 119
quiet, 60, 99

R

raped, 103
reality shows, 55
reap, 108
rebel, 70, 97
rebellion, 4, 27, 70
rebellious, 94
receive, 22, 46, 53, 60, 64, 72, 73, 76, 90, 91
reciprocity, 108
reckless life, 43
recover, 3
rededicate, 43
refuge, 26
refused, 24, 58, 64, 109
regardless, 2, 23, 89, 113, 115
regretted, 3
reject, 12, 13
rejoice, 31
relationship, 3, 20, 38, 40, 88
remarried, 70
remembrance, 25
rent, 64
repent, 4, 21, 27, 33, 40, 43, 50, 56, 70, 108
repented, 32, 38, 64

replacement, 20

representation, 62, 91

reproach, 10, 31, 32, 59, 77

reputable, 107

reputations, 67

resolve, 77

resolved, 88

respectfully, 113

responsibility, 4, 40, 105, 113

rest, 5, 16, 18, 25, 48, 87, 119

restitution, 52

restoration, 6, 98

restored, 2, 3, 32, 100

reveal, 1, 65

revelation, 69, 97

riches, 83, 125

right path, 54

righteous, 26

rock bottom, 11

routine, 115

rude, 113, 125

ruin, 67, 118

ruined, 105

rulers of darkness, 56

S

safeguards, 128
Saint, 37
sales, 82
salvation, 34, 128
Samuel, 19, 20, 88
Satan, 22, 24, 29, 111
Saturday, 37
Saul, 19, 20
saved, 43, 81, 97, 127
Savior, 114
scandal, 31, 83
scandals, 11, 81, 108, 128
school, 32, 67, 103, 122
scorner, 12
scorners, 48
scorning,, 48
Scripture, 4, 113
season, 48, 49, 51, 82, 116
Season, 83
Secret, 132
secular counselor, 49
secure, 54
self-deliverance, 2
selfish, 50, 88
self-sufficient, 63

seminars, 63, 82
servant, 22, 131
servants, 6
service, 102
sex, 42, 67, 125, 128
shame, 13, 32, 33, 46, 51, 52, 53, 64, 72, 94, 95
shock, 1
shoebox, 103
shortcomings, 33, 100
siblings, 79
sick, 76, 97, 109, 115, 127
side chick, 100
sight, 9, 21, 25, 37, 38, 40, 69
silly mistakes, 12, 13
simpletons, 48
sin, 8, 9, 11, 12, 13, 20, 22, 23, 25, 32, 37, 38, 40, 42, 43, 45, 58, 70, 74, 84, 97, 112, 116, 128
sincere, 38
sinful, 25, 105, 113
sinned, 103
sinners, 28
sins, 4, 31, 32, 37, 51, 80, 108
situation, 12, 64, 79, 89, 94, 114
six feet under, 103
sky, 28, 40
slander, 14, 66

Index

slave of righteousness, 100
sleepless nights, 97
snare, 17, 102
social media, 15, 56, 58, 76, 82, 100, 113, 125, 128
social media networks, 15, 58, 82
soda, 67, 76
soft answer, 55
solution, 69, 81
sorrow, 14, 16, 60, 96
soul, 17, 26, 100, 102, 119, 122, 126
souls, 30, 42, 81
South Carolina, 131
sovereign, 59
sow, 108
spared, 29, 46, 93, 103
speak, 2, 8, 10, 17, 24, 39, 40, 49, 69, 72, 91, 100, 109
speech, 61, 83
spheres, 57
Spirit, 5, 6, 8, 11, 14, 25, 56, 71, 86, 124, 126
Spirit of God, 6
spirit of sabotage, 116
spirit of seduction, 61, 125
spirits, 5, 38, 54, 85
spouses, 88

stake, 78

stalk, 78

stars, 28

STDs, 42, 43

steadfast spirit, 92

steal, 58, 112

steps, 7, 38, 44, 53, 71, 97, 100

steward, 111, 113

stigma, 57

stomped, 67

stores, 64

storm, 65

story, 82

strangers, 35

strength, 25, 46, 53, 80, 89

strengthened, 26

strengths, 27, 37

stress, 96, 97

stressors, 48

strife, 16, 17, 107, 108

Strongholds, 132

stubborn, 64, 85

study, 6

stumble, 11, 31, 62, 75, 129

stumbling block, 10, 23

stupid, 23, 24, 34, 51

Index

stupidity, 78
Styrofoam, 103
submitted, 93, 116
succeed, 68
successful, 35
sucked, 125
suffer, 24, 29, 73, 121
suffering, 25, 39
sun, 28
Sunday, 37
Supernatural, 132
supernatural acceleration, 53
supporters, 82
suppress, 100
suppressed, 88
swallow, 78

T

tangible, 29
teachable, 12, 50
tear down, 7
Tears, 2
teenager, 67, 97, 102
temple, 5, 39
temptation, 38

test, 20, 48, 116, 117
testament, 35
tested, 76
testimonies, 6, 131
testimony, 3, 82
testing, 20
Thank You, 26, 27, 30, 33, 41, 44, 47, 50, 53, 56, 59, 62, 65, 68, 71, 74, 80, 83, 89, 92, 95, 97, 98, 100, 101, 103, 106, 108, 111, 114, 120, 123, 129
thankful, 2, 46
thoughts, 1, 10, 39
threaten, 78
threatened, 79, 103
thresholds, 84
timberland, 102
tired, 6, 20, 33, 59, 86, 110
title, 82, 113
tongue, 16, 90
tongues, 29, 78
torch, 35
tormented, 38
toxic environment, 115
toxic people, 12
track, 64, 84, 116
traffic, 122
training, 63

Index

transformative power, 33
transgression, 10, 42
transgressions, 31, 33
translates, 45
treating, 113
trees, 28
trials, 28, 39, 65
Tron, 131
trouble, 3, 23, 60, 61, 81, 83, 109
trust, 15, 20, 56, 89
Trust, 2, 122
truth, 29, 74, 104, 108, 124, 126
turmoil, 35
TV, 67
tweet, 107
twisting, 104

U

unbeliever, 30
unclean spirit, 5
understanding, 13, 54, 87, 99
unforgiveness, 4
unteachable, 25
upholding, 105
uprightly, 80, 117

upset, 58, 73, 84, 88, 103, 119
utilities, 64

V

vapor, 34
vengeance, 80, 116
verbal agreements, 102
Verse, 19, 22, 25, 28, 31, 34, 37, 39, 42, 45, 48, 51, 54, 57, 63, 66, 69, 72, 75, 78, 81, 87, 90, 93, 96, 99, 102, 107, 109, 112, 115, 118, 121, 127
vessel, 108
Vice President, 82
victim mentality, 105
videos, 29
vindicate, 26, 58
visions, 69
voice, 28, 69, 130
vomit, 17, 115
vulnerable, 69

W

warfare, 26, 75
Warfare, 132
warn, 54, 70, 108, 109

warning, 115
watching, 55, 58, 79
watered, 29
weaknesses, 37, 75
wealth, 34, 35, 51
weary, 8, 127
Weary, 133
wedlock, 42
wicked, 5, 9, 16, 18, 23, 24, 26, 39, 40, 60, 73, 84, 85, 86, 121, 125
wickedness, 126
wife, 23, 88
wilderness, 49, 64
wisdom, 4, 7, 10, 12, 16, 24, 30, 35, 45, 46, 53, 65, 83, 85, 87, 93, 100, 109, 123
Wisdom, 87, 132
wise, 4, 6, 14, 15, 16, 30, 34, 35, 51, 60, 63, 65, 69, 70, 72, 78, 81, 84, 90, 99, 127
witnessed, 107
womb, 1, 2
women, 2, 22, 23, 57, 100, 128, 130
wonders, 30, 131
Word of God, 127
Work, 132
workers of iniquity, 25, 125
Workforce, 132

world, 2, 75, 77, 102, 122, 127, 130
worse, 5, 16, 109
worship, 40
worthy, 6, 33
wrath, 15, 55, 72, 124
wreck, 74, 112
written, 102
wrong crowd, 51, 122
wrong ones, 46
wrong path, 54
wrong spirit, 70

Y

yawning, 2
yielded, 52
Yoke, 131
young lady, 70, 82, 91

www.ingramcontent.com/pod-product-compliance
Lightning Source LLC
Chambersburg PA
CBHW072010110526
44592CB00012B/1260